CW01497587

DayOne
'The LORD is a man of war.'
(Exodus 15:3)
'With us is the LORD our God to help us, and to fight our battles.'
(2 Chronicles 32:8)

(this spread) Soldiers of the 1st Battalion The Rifles based in Chepstow, Gloucester, on exercise in the Sennybridge Training Area, Powys, Wales, 2018

(previous page) The battleship USS Iowa fires a full 'broadside' of all its big guns, including nine 15 inch guns (38cm diameter shells weighing 880kg / 1938lbs), off Puerto Rico in 1984. 15in shells can be fired 19 miles / 30km

Discover.
Learn.
Live.
Lessons
for
Life
BATTLE SCHOOL
Mark Philpott

Attention: orders for new recruits

When I was young and naive, growing up in the 1970s, I used to love tanks, warships and fighter planes, and I dreamt of being in Her Majesty's Armed Forces. My mum and dad had uncles who had fought in the World Wars, some of which I knew quite well. I loved attending army barracks open days, Navy Days at Chatham and Portsmouth, and the Royal Tournament military tattoo in London. I lived in my green army jumper, covered with stickers!

As I grew older (and hopefully wiser), I learnt that war is horrible, and so many people suffer even today in wars around the world. We are truly blessed if we have only lived in peacetime. And yet I also learnt that sometimes wars must be fought to defend life and freedom – it may be the right thing to do.

The Bible is the real history of the world from the very beginning. It tells us that God made Man, and then Man sinned when he disobeyed God in the Garden of Eden. This brought pride and conflict into the world, and men have been fighting ever since. The Bible is full of stories of battles and the exploits of warriors like Joshua, David and Jonathan.

We all find life a struggle sometimes, because the world and our human nature have been ruined by sin. The New Testament part of the Bible tells us that Christians are daily in a battle: not an outward battle fighting with swords or guns, but an inward battle; a struggle to do the right thing, to resist temptation, and to keep looking to and loving Jesus no matter what.

In this book you will find out about the battle of life, learn about the military, and, I hope, understand something about Jesus' victory in the biggest battle of all.

Mark Philpott 2025

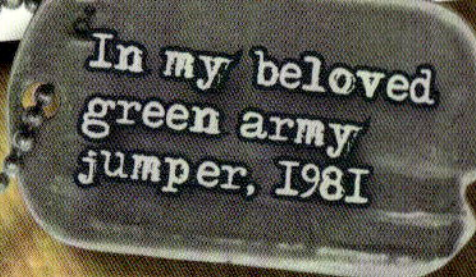

In my beloved green army jumper, 1981

Great Uncle Cyril, Lance Corporal, Royal Horse Artillery in WWI

Great Uncle Billy, Seaforth Highlanders, served in North Africa in WW2

Great Uncle Reg was in the SAS, but no-one in the family knew for years

Gt. Uncle Harold, a paratrooper dropped as part of Operation Market Garden

On a Royal Navy ship docked next to HMS Apollo, Portsmouth Navy Day, 1977

Attending RAF Swinderby for my friend Andy's Passing Out Parade 1990

97 Sqn Air Training Corps, Mitcham Road Barracks, 1986

Eden Camp museum, former Prisoner of War Camp, Malton, nr. York, 2019

On the Death Railway, Thailand (built by POWs 1942–3), 1996

Trip to Belgium to see First World War cemeteries, memorials and trenches, 2004

In airworthy Spitfire IX TA805 'Spirit of Kent', Biggin Hill, 2021

Before you start . . . get a Bible

As you read this book, look up the Bible quotes given in the brown boxes. God's words are much wiser than mine! If you don't have a 'real' Bible, see if you can download one, or go online.

CONTENTS

Battle School Curriculum

A 'Green Beret' Royal Marine Commando looks down the sights of his weapon

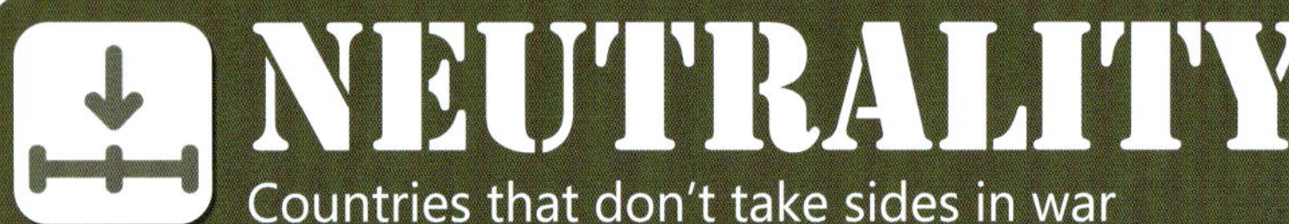

NEUTRALITY
Countries that don't take sides in war

"Leave me out of it!"

Some nations, like Switzerland and Sweden, decided to stay out of the two World Wars and be on neither one side or the other. Such nations are said to be **neutral**. How can this be? A country is only safe if all parties in a war respect the 'Law of Neutrality' in international law. Because warring countries sometimes don't respect international law, neutral nations usually have their own armed forces to deter would-be aggressors.

Switzerland found themselves in a very difficult situation in WW2 and some have questioned how neutral they really were. Before and during the war, the Allies and the Nazis both banked in Switzerland because the Swiss currency was linked to the price of gold, and so would hold its value. War is expensive so a good bank is vital. By 1940, Switzerland was surrounded by Nazi-occupied countries. Why didn't Hitler invade? The Swiss kept talking to Hitler because they relied on coal from Germany to stay warm and provide power, and they came to some sort of understanding. The Swiss had a railway running under the Alps which connected Germany with Italy, and if Hitler had invaded, the Swiss would have blown it up. In exchange for coal they allowed war materials to be transported on their railway. They also did certain things to avoid upsetting the Nazis, which we may consider wrong. But we weren't there so maybe it is best to not judge after the fact, and without all the information.

THE BIBLE SAYS...

Jesus said, 'He that is not with me is against me.' (Matthew 12:30)

LEARNING POINT

The Second World War (WW2) involved most nations on Earth. It was the most total, deadly, global war there has been to date. And yet some countries did manage to stay out of it. There is a spiritual war which has been raging since the Garden of Eden (Genesis 3:15) and it will continue until the end of time (Matthew 24:21-23). Jesus said that no-one will be able to stay neutral in this spiritual war. We are either on God's side or Satan's side, whether we want to be involved or not. Are you on the Lord's side? (Exodus 32:26)

Prior to joining NATO, Sweden took neutrality so seriously that it developed its own fighters so it would not be dependent on others; here is the Saab Draken (top left), Viggen (left) and Gripen (above)

The Swiss Air Force has air bases in the Alps with hangars built into the rocks. This is an F/A-18C Hornet departing Meiringen Air Base

DID YOU KNOW?

Switzerland has not been in a war since 1505. It has the oldest policy of being neutral in war, established in 1815 when Napoleon abdicated, although there was Civil War in 1847

ALLIANCES

Military agreements with other nations

DID YOU KNOW?
NATO is also called the North Atlantic Alliance

NATO (blue) and Warsaw Pact (red) countries during the Cold War

NATO MEMBERS IN 2025

- Albania
- Belgium
- Bulgaria
- Canada
- Croatia
- Czech Republic
- Denmark
- Estonia
- Finland
- France
- Germany
- Greece
- Hungary
- Iceland
- Italy
- Latvia
- Lithuania
- Luxembourg
- Montenegro
- Netherlands
- N. Macedonia
- Norway
- Poland
- Portugal
- Romania
- Slovakia
- Slovenia
- Spain
- Sweden
- Turkey
- UK
- USA

Are you in with a good crowd?

An alliance may be defined as 'a relationship among people, groups or states that have joined together for mutual benefit or to achieve a common purpose.' Military alliances have been common down through the ages because there is wisdom in having friends who can help you in times of trouble. When nations are *allied* with each other, it can deter would-be aggressors from invading because they would have to overcome all nations involved. However, alliances can cause a war to grow wildly out of control. Before WW1, nations on both sides had made agreements to protect each other in the event of invasion or war being declared; but ironically this led to a rapid expansion of the war across and beyond Europe.

After WW2, the Soviets under Stalin had plans to rule all of Eastern Europe and there was fear that they would try to conquer the whole of Europe. The 'Cold War' had begun with both sides suspicious of each other. As a result, in 1949 the nations of Western Europe, with the US, formed a new alliance called NATO (North Atlantic Treaty Organisation) and the Soviets led the Warsaw Pact (a union of nations under their influence). After the Soviet Union collapsed in 1991, many have questioned why NATO still exists and whether there have been times when it has caused wars or made them worse—such as in the Balkans (1992-95) and Ukraine.

NATO summits in Washington DC, USA (2024) and Brussels (2023)

LEARNING POINT

Alliances may be right or wrong. It is very important who you choose for friends! Will they be watching out for your good? Or will they lead you astray and get you into trouble? The Bible gives several instances of good and bad choices; David made both—'good' with Jonathan (1 Samuel 18:1) and 'bad' with Achish (1 Samuel 21:10-15, 27:1-3, 29:1-2). Jehoshaphat was the godly King of Judah who made an alliance with the wicked King Ahab of Israel and God was angry with him for it (2 Chronicles 18:1-3, 19:1-3).

Christians making friends with other Christians will be a blessing to each other (Romans 12:10, Hebrews 10:24). But the most important 'alliance' to enter wisely is marriage. The Bible is very clear that believers should not be joined to unbelievers (2 Corinthians 6:14). Solomon is an excellent example of how even the wisest man who has ever lived could make foolish decisions. He married women from pagan (ungodly) nations, and his wives turned him away from worshipping the one true God (1 Kings 11:1-13). Praise the LORD, though, that he was still a forgiven child of God and is now in Heaven despite his foolish alliances! It is never too late to turn away from sinful ways. Ultimately, our trust and safety should always be in God, not Man.

THE BIBLE SAYS . . .

'Woe unto them that go down to Egypt for help ... and trust in chariots ... and horsemen, because they are very strong; but they look not unto the ... LORD. ... The Egyptians are men, and not God." (Isaiah 31:1,3)

A photo perfectly capturing the attitudes of Stalin (Soviet Union), Roosevelt (USA) and Churchill (UK)—leaders of the main Allied nations in WW2—at a conference in 1943. Churchill wanted to maintain the British Empire whilst Roosevelt wanted to end it; and Stalin was a brutal dictator who neither the UK or USA would normally have tolerated. Yet the Nazi threat was considered so severe that the UK became allied with both

RECRUITMENT

Joining the military

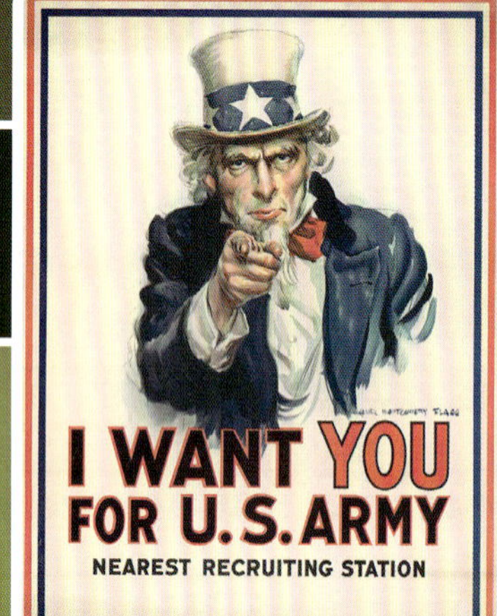

I WANT YOU
FOR U.S. ARMY
NEAREST RECRUITING STATION

US poster of 'Uncle Sam' used in WW1, similar to the famous British image of Lord Kitchener, 'Your Country Needs You'

Signing your life away

Modern armed forces put a lot of effort into persuading young men (and increasingly women) to 'join up.' This includes promotional events at colleges and universities, running cadet groups, advertising campaigns, attending public events with display teams and helping at major sporting occasions such as the Wimbledon tennis tournament and the FA Cup Final at Wembley.

Between about 1664 and the early 1800s, much more brutal tactics were used during wartime by the British Royal Navy. They became infamous for 'press-gangs' which would hunt around coastal areas and by force take men onto ships to become sailors. Almost unbelievably, the law courts in England defended the Navy's right to do this, saying it was vital for the war effort!

During the French Revolution in the 1790s, young men were legally bound to sign up and serve from across the country, which created a very large army. Known as 'national conscription,' this was copied by other European nations and was used extensively during WW1 and WW2.

LEARNING POINT

Every Christian is a soldier in the army of the Lord Jesus Christ. Is that because they were born into a Christian family, and so automatically became a believer? Is it because their parents forced them into it? No, because the Bible, in John 1:12-13, says that no-one becomes God's by 'blood' (family) or 'the will of man' (being forced or persuaded). There is no forced conscription or press-gang to get someone to be a Christian.

So does God make being a Christian fun, exciting or well paid, to persuade men, women, boys and girls to 'join up?' No, because Jesus promises a life of hardship and suffering for those who follow Him (Matthew 10:22,34). How then is anyone a Christian?

The Bible makes it clear that everyone who follows Jesus and joins His army is willing because God has put it in their heart (Psalm 110:3, John 6:44). The Holy Spirit convicts each one that they are a sinner who needs Jesus as Saviour. They love and follow Him even to death (John 13:37).

THE BIBLE SAYS...

'Breath came into them, and they lived, and stood upon their feet, an exceeding great army.' (Ezekiel 37:10)

'No man can come to me [Jesus], except the Father ... draw him.' (John 6:44)

DID YOU KNOW?
Between 1949 and 1960, young British men were required to do up to two years National Service

(main image) The RAF Red Arrows displaying off Bournemouth beach, 2022; note the Red Arrows promotional bus at the bottom of the photo; (left) The Royal Marines Commando Display Team demonstrate a beach assault, also at Bournemouth; (below) The RAF Falcons Parachute Display Team

CONSCIENTIOUS OBJECTORS

Those who refuse to join up because they think it is wrong to go to war

Is it right to fight? Is there a 'Just war'?

Should Christians kill others? Wasn't Jesus clear about loving even your enemy, when He spoke to His disciples?

These are questions which have been much debated since the days of the early Church, when in general Christians were anti-war based on Jesus' teachings (Luke 6:27). However, when Christians began to have positions in authority after Constantine came to power in the Roman Empire, they could use their position to stop bad things happening, and protect their citizens from enemies. Was it right to sit back and do nothing? Or was it right to use force to protect the innocent?

Augustine of Hippo

Augustine of Hippo (354-430 AD) was an early 'Church Father' whose teachings remained important down to the Protestant Reformation and are to this day. Although saying that Christians should be *pacifists* (see inset right) in their personal life, he argued that there is such a thing as a 'Just war' (e.g. Eccles. 3:8). He said that wanting peace must include the option of fighting to preserve it. A war must only be defensive, he said. But does this include defending those abroad who are being attacked, who are friends with you? Or only those who you are responsible for? The Bible is not a detailed handbook of running a country and many areas of life are left to personal conscience. The words of Jesus to Peter in John 21:21-22 indicate that if the Bible does not give *specific* directions, a Christian must listen to his/her own conscience and not judge others for their decisions.

Pacifist

... is the term used for someone who is <u>against</u> war and violence. The symbol above, designed in 1958 for a campaign to rid Britain of nuclear weapons, is often associated with pacifism. Before that, a dove with an olive leaf was used (a reference to Noah).

Since WW2, public anti-war marches have been organised by political groups, especially socialists who may have been using pacifism as an excuse to bring down capitalist governments. Pacifism is often seen as being wrong or naive by veterans, families of war-dead, and arguably most Christians.

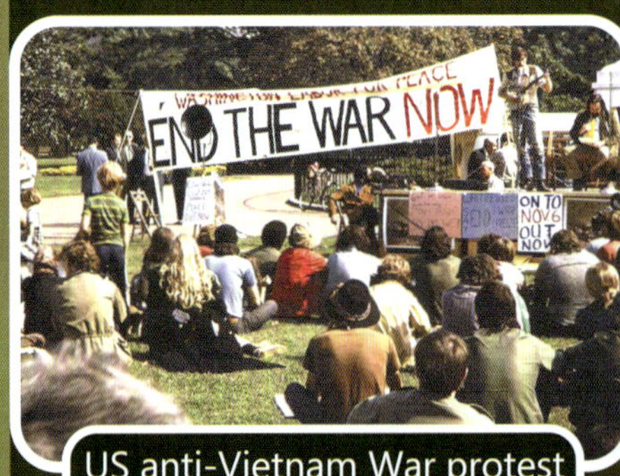

US anti-Vietnam War protest

A man who objects to serving in the military, because his conscience says that he shouldn't, is known as a ***conscientious objector***. In the past, they were often Christians of one group or another. The right to be a conscientious objector is now recognised in various laws and agreements, but as recently as WW1, men were compelled to serve against their conscience. An example of this is the story of four Strict Baptist brothers from Birkenhead, near Liverpool, who were taken to court because they would not join up when conscripted. They lost their case and were either put into prison or forced to serve. At that time, it was generally seen as a disgrace to not go to war, and sometimes men in civilian clothing were shamed by women who would pin a white feather on them as a sign of being a coward. Tragically a few men then committed suicide.

The White Feather Movement in WW1 (and WW2)

There is also another group of Christians who will not take life but who believe the war may be a just cause, or want to care for their fellow countrymen whilst doing no harm to others. These can best be described as *conscientious co-operators*.

A number of Christians who objected to carrying a gun joined medical units in WW1 and WW2 as they were unarmed, focusing on saving life (see **pp66-67**)

Propaganda has played a key role in shaping public opinion about whether a war is right to fight. Even Christians can get caught up in the lies and half-truths of politicians.

LEARNING POINT

As we become more mature, it is good if we know what we believe and to have a clear idea about right and wrong grounded on the teaching in the Bible. Our views can change over time, perhaps by listening to people with other points of view. Personally, in the past, I have been very judgemental about conscientious objectors who would not fight in WW1 or WW2, believing Britain had a just cause. In WW2, the UK declared war to free Poland from the Nazis; but the Allies ultimately let Poland be under oppressive Soviet Communist control after the war. The war led to immense suffering and 100+ million dead. Was it right and worthwhile? Most say "Yes," some say "No." Was it right to invade countries in the Middle East after 9/11 (the New York 'Twin Towers' attack, 2001) in the name of a "war on terror," or were those wars really about money and power? Do we have all the information? Should we be more careful in judging someone else's conscience?

THE BIBLE SAYS . . .

'Judge [discern] not according to the appearance [how it looks], but judge righteous judgement.' (John 7:24)

BASIC TRAINING

Recruits getting used to military life in 'Boot Camp'

"You're in the Army now!"

Every new recruit joining the armed forces has to go through several weeks of 'basic (or initial) training.' This is necessary to shape them into useful instruments who will obey orders and work together as a team at all times. There is strict discipline, normally dished out by an unpleasant drill sergeant, who will do everything he can to make the new recruits' lives miserable until they do everything right. This is important because in combat, (*cont'd next page*)

All images on this page from the USA: (main image) US Marine recruits get a taste of a drill instructor on their first route march; (images left) Assault courses build courage, strength and a determination to succeed; (above) Someone's in trouble; (below) parade ground inspection

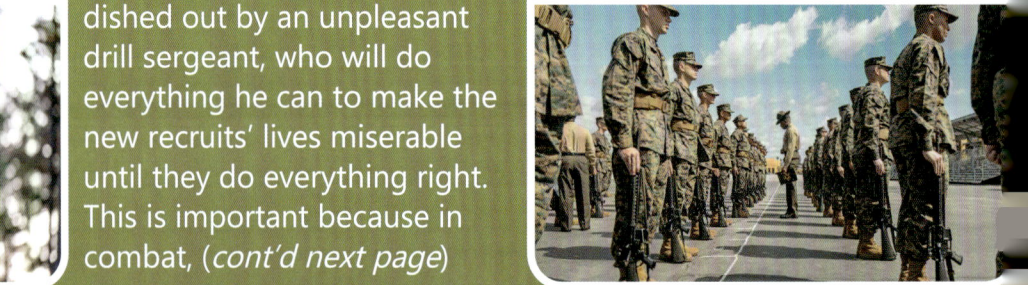

it could be the difference between life and death. Basic training is intended to be exhausting and push individuals to their limits so they realise just how much they can do if they need to. Wartime is extremely tiring, dangerous and harsh, and soldiers need to be prepared.

Another aspect of basic training is to keep the recruits very busy from morning to bedtime, so they don't think too much about the comfortable home and loving family they may have left behind. Too much time to think might cause them to change their mind and not be committed to the challenging life before them.

DID YOU KNOW?
Royal Marine Commandos' initial training is one of the longest and toughest in the world, at 32 weeks. On 'passing out' they earn the coveted *green beret*

BASIC TRAINING: WHAT TO EXPECT

» Early starts; food rations; night exercises; room, bed and kit inspections; boot polishing and uniform washing/ironing
» Lots of physical exercise including assault courses, route marches with backpacks and rifles, and circuit training
» Confidence and skill building including hand-to-hand combat, gun maintenance, marksmanship on the shooting range, and survival in the wild
» Team building and obedience training by marching and rifle drill on the parade ground; punishments for mistakes including push-ups, running around the parade ground, cleaning duty etc.

LEARNING POINT

Shortly after arriving at camp, recruits can find it a hard experience. They are likely to have their head shaved, be given an uncomfortable uniform to wear, a number to be known by, and have to share a room with a dozen or more others. They need determination to stay and finish the course, remembering the reasons why they joined, and not quit and go back to their old way of life which was more comfortable.

So it is for new believers when they follow Christ as His disciple. Jesus said that anyone who puts their family or self before Him cannot be a real, true disciple (Matthew 10:37). Jesus must come first. The cost, in leaving behind old ways and old pleasures, has to be counted. But the end will be worth it! (Matthew 19:29)

The US Navy display team flies over a sailors' graduation ceremony, Annapolis, Maryland, 2020

THE BIBLE SAYS . . .
'I [Paul] count all things but loss for the excellency of the knowledge of Christ ... that I may win Christ.' (Philippians 3:8)
Read Luke 14:26-33; Philippians 3:13-14

UNIFORMS

Military clothing identifying who you belong to

DID YOU KNOW?
Khaki is an Urdu/Persian word for 'soil-coloured.' It is now a common colour for uniforms and civilian clothing. It ranges from pale brown to a drab green

Whose side are you on?

In ancient times, warriors wore the clothing of their tribe or culture. Although the army of the Roman Empire wore recognisable armour, there was no consistency. The first widespread use of standardised military uniforms intended to be *uniform* (planned to have no variation) began with the French when they organised the army into regiments in the mid-1600s. It was the English Civil War (1642-51) which first saw widespread use by opposing armies. A benefit of uniforms supplied by the King, Emperor or President was to show which side you were fighting for.

English Civil War re-enactment

Until the mid-1800s, tactics were to stand in close groups; bright colours were ideal for being identified in the smoke of battle to avoid *friendly fire* (see **p62**), and were good for encouraging a sense of belonging or identity by all dressing the same within the unit. From the mid-1800s, when smokeless gunpowder allowed soldiers to hide and not be spotted when firing, khaki started to be worn by the British Army in India to camouflage troops. Since WW1, battle dress has nearly always been in camouflage—drab colours and, more recently, patterned—to blend in with their surroundings. Traditional brightly coloured outfits are reserved for special (ceremonial) occasions.

LEARNING POINT

What clothing do Christians wear in Jesus' army? Are they identified by what clothes they put on? Not generally. The warfare is not natural (seen) but spiritual (unseen), so the clothing will not be what you can see with your eyes. The Apostle Paul says that to be ready for the spiritual battle, all Christians should wear the same things, which he lists in Ephesians 6:14-17. But most importantly, Christians <u>all</u> wear the identical (*uniform*) robe of Christ's perfection (Isaiah 61:10) provided by the King of kings; that is, Jesus covers their sin with His own perfect life. This clothing is a gift from God; it cannot be bought or made by us (Ephesians 2:8).

THE BIBLE SAYS . . .
'I will greatly rejoice in the LORD, my soul shall be joyful in my God; for he *has* clothed me with the garments of salvation, he *has* covered me with the robe of righteousness.' (Isaiah 61:10)

(main image) A Welsh Guard wearing the famous bearskin (hat) and red coat

(below left to right) Roman soldier wearing segmented armour; soldiers wearing the famous Scottish 'Black Watch' tartan kilts; British WW2 battle dress; modern US camouflage

Soldiers carrying SA80 rifles of the Household Division amass on Horse Guards Parade in central London near Buckingham Palace to rehearse for the King's official Birthday celebration 'Trooping the Colour,' 2023

Who is on the Lord's side? Who will serve the King?
    Who will be His helpers, other lives to bring?
Who will leave the world's side? Who will face the foe?
    Who is on the Lord's side? Who for Him will go?
By Thy call of mercy, by Thy grace divine,
    We are on the Lord's side—Saviour, we are Thine!

Not for weight of glory, nor for crown and palm,
    Enter we the army, raise the warrior psalm;
But for love that claimeth lives for whom He died:
    He whom Jesus saveth marches on His side.
By Thy love constraining, by Thy grace divine,
    We are on the Lord's side—Saviour, we are Thine!

Fierce may be the conflict, strong may be the foe,
    But the King's own army none can overthrow;
Around His standard ranging, victory is secure,
    For His truth unchanging makes the triumph sure.
Joyfully enlisting, by Thy grace divine,
    We are on the Lord's side—Saviour, we are Thine!

Chosen to be soldiers, in a foreign land,
    Chosen, called, and faithful, for our Captain's band;
In the service royal, let us not grow cold,
    Let us be right loyal, noble, true and bold.
Master, wilt Thou keep us, by Thy grace divine,
    Always on the Lord's side—Saviour, always Thine!

This hymn by (Miss) Frances Havergal (1836-1879), whilst not mentioning wearing a uniform, speaks of being ready to be identified as one of the Lord's soldiers, no matter the personal cost.

The hymn is based on the account of Moses coming down Mount Sinai and finding that the Children of Israel had so quickly forgotten the LORD God.

THE BIBLE SAYS . . .
'Then Moses stood in the gate of the camp, and said, Who is on the LORD's side? let him come unto me.' (Exodus 32:26)

RANK

Military hierarchy

DID YOU KNOW?
When personnel salute an officer, it is the rank (position) they are recognising, not the person

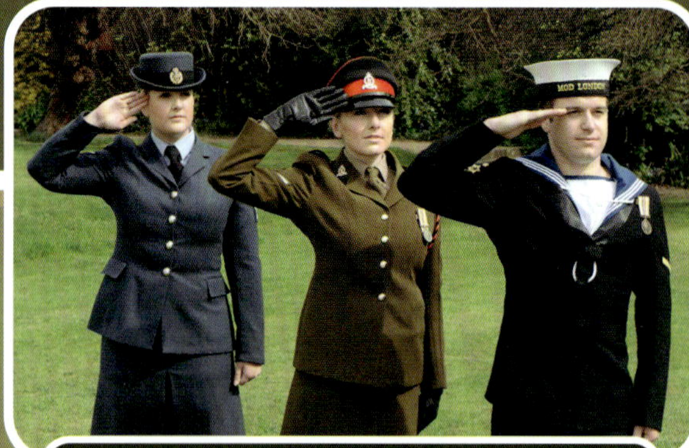

Members of the RAF, Army and Royal Navy (RN) salute. The RN posture was adopted because historically sailors had dirty hands from scrubbing the ship's deck, so angled their palms downward

Know your place

An army is a force used by a king, president or other controlling body to fulfil their will using force; the orders ultimately come right from the top. So how can a body of thousands or millions of combatants be directed effectively? There must be a structure in the organisation so that high level orders can be passed down to someone who decides what should be done. The decision then needs putting into practice by 'boots on the ground.'

Most armed forces manage this through senior ranks called 'officers' who are appointed directly with what is called a 'commission.' All other personnel below them are called 'other ranks'. Those in the 'other ranks' can be promoted and become Non-Commissioned Officers (NCOs), which are junior officers still below the level of the commissioned officers. NCOs include Corporals and Sergeants who are the men (and women) in charge of the most junior ranks and provide leadership day-to-day amongst their platoon, squadron or unit.

In many armed forces, senior officers wear a gold braid on their peaks; these officers may be referred to as those 'with scrambled egg(s) on their hats'

The rank structure in the British Army is shown opposite. Rank is shown through a combination of shoulder flashes (called epaulettes), badges on the arm (or wrist bands for Royal Navy officers, see photo left), and markings on peaked caps for officers. Officers in uniform should always be saluted by junior ranks. Failure to do so may result in a punishment as maintaining discipline and rank is viewed as critical to avoid a collapse of discipline, leading to orders being ignored and reducing the ability to wage war as a reliable, united force.

LEARNING POINT

In days past, the word 'salute' or 'salutation' was used to simply mean a *greeting*. When Paul tells Christians to greet ('salute') one another in Romans 16:16, he is telling them to do so out of loving respect, and not because any one person is more important. The only ranks in the Christian church are elders/pastors,

deacons, and saints (Philippians 1:1). The Bible is clear: those in authority in the local church are to be obeyed (Hebrews 13:17), while those older in years are to be respected by the young (1 Peter 5:5). However, Jesus washed His disciples' feet—the dirty job of a servant—to show that every Christian must put others first and themselves last, no matter who they are (Romans 12:10).

THE BIBLE SAYS . . .
'If I then being your Lord and Master, have washed your feet, ... wash one another's feet.' (John 13:14)

TRAINING EXERCISES

Peacetime practice to ensure combat readiness

DID YOU KNOW?
Military exercises can be called 'war games'

Are you ready?

A war can start with virtually no warning. When Argentina invaded the British territory of the Falkland Islands on 2 April 1982, the UK Government only found out the Argentinian plans 24 hours beforehand. Likewise, the Japanese attack on Pearl Harbour has been held up as an example of a surprise attack (though some believe the US knew in advance). It is therefore vital for a military force to **be ready and able**; to be prepared at all times, and vigilant in looking for potential threats. Being capable in the military does not just happen by chance. It takes practice.

It is vital that military personnel build physical strength and endurance, work well together, develop effective tactics and master the use of equipment. Whilst some of this can be done in basic training, most of the capability is built during specially arranged training exercises. These are usually mock (simulated) battle scenarios, with some of the military playing the part of an enemy. The exercises normally involve firing weapons, sometimes with 'live' ammunition (that is, not 'blanks' which would do no harm). Western nations, typically those who are members of NATO, hold joint exercises in a range of locations around Europe and in the North Atlantic. These test their ability to work together despite having different languages, tactics and systems. The ability to work together is known as 'interoperability.'

Dogs and handlers of 102 Military Working Dogs Sqn. taking part in a live fire exercise in Germany, 2016

LEARNING POINT

Can you just pick something up and immediately be an expert using it? No! (1 Samuel 17:39) It takes a lot of regular use to become skilful. There is no point having equipment without being able to use it like second nature. In the military it is a matter of life and death, and so it is in a Christian's life. Paul says that he/she is to take 'the whole armour of God' including the 'shield of faith' and the 'sword of the Spirit,' and to be 'praying always' (Ephesians 6:10-18). Why does he say this? It is to be **prepared** for Satan's attacks which come against anyone who loves Jesus Christ. Faith, prayer and the Bible aren't just for Sundays; they are to be a daily exercise.

(top) US soldiers from the 101st Airborne Division and Romanian troops in combined land/air training, Romania, 2022; (inset) Commandos in an inflatable boat board a Royal Navy submarine during an exercise in Norway, 2022; (bottom) An RAF Typhoon takes off from a public road during an exercise in Finland, 2023

THE BIBLE SAYS . . .

'Blessed be the LORD my strength, which *trains* my hands *for* war.' (Psalm 144:1)

'Be ready to [do] every good work.' (Titus 3:1)

06

(left) Soldiers abseil from Romanian IAR-330 (Puma) helicopters during NATO exercise Steadfast Defender in 2021

(right) A Challenger 2 tank of the British Army churns up huge dust clouds during Steadfast Defender 2024, in Poland

(below right) Royal Marines from 47 Commando train in a newly upgraded raiding craft, Plymouth Sound, 2024

DID YOU KNOW?

The largest NATO exercise since the Cold War (Steadfast Defender 2024) involved over 90,000 troops coming from all NATO countries

WEAPONS OF WAR

The development of fighting tools

DID YOU KNOW?
King Uzziah of Judah (790-739BC) was amongst the first to employ machines for firing arrows and rocks (2 Chronicles 26:15)

The race for better and better weapons

Man is different from the animal kingdom in that he has been created with sufficient intelligence to devise and make tools. From the earliest times, Man's ability to smelt rocks to make items out of metal has led to the development of a wide range of powerful weapons. Wartime has seen the biggest technical leaps as craftsmen, engineers and scientists work extra hard to invent and produce weapons which can give an advantage over the enemy.

(below, both pages) Some of the key weapon developments through the ages

Swords, spears, lances etc.

Horse-drawn chariot

Projectile firing machines

Cannon, gunpowder

Fully-automatic machine gun

Rifled artillery gun

The ultimate weapon of war today is the long-range guided nuclear missile.

LEARNING POINT

But there is an even more powerful weapon, the ultimate weapon which will never be bettered and against which there is no defence. This is the 'sword of the Spirit', which is the Word of God the Bible (Ephesians 6:17) and it is also Jesus Himself (John 1:1). Why is the Word of God described as more lethal than the sharpest sword? It is because it can cut right into our thoughts and feelings, not just into the body. It gets to the heart of who we are as sinners in the sight of a holy God; it brings men and women, boys and girls to 'be killed' to their old lives of pleasing self, but then it makes them alive again with a new, better life to serve a loving God.

Read Deuteronomy 32:39, Matthew 10:34, Romans 6:4, Revelation 1:16.

THE BIBLE SAYS ...

'For the word of God is *living* and powerful, and sharper than any two-edged sword, piercing even to the *separation* of soul and spirit, ... and is a discerner of the thoughts and intents of the heart.' (Hebrews 4:12)

1910s
Battle tank

1930s
Heavy bomber

1940s
Flying bomb (stand-off weapon)

Jet fighter-bombers

1940s

Nuclear bomb

1940s

Long-range nuclear missile

1950s

S.A.S.R.A.

The Sword of the Spirit in the UK's Armed Forces

DID YOU KNOW?
There are a number of other Christian organisations serving the UK Armed Forces including The Naval and Military Bible Society

The Soldiers' and Aviators' Scripture Readers Association

The verse on the SASRA logo contain the words of Jesus telling his hearers to 'be ready' to meet God, because no-one knows when that will be. This is especially important for serving military personnel as they may suddenly come into life-threatening situations.

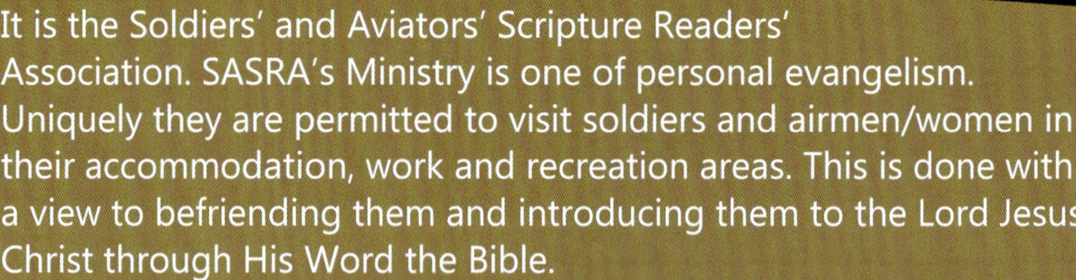

What is SASRA?

It is the Soldiers' and Aviators' Scripture Readers' Association. SASRA's Ministry is one of personal evangelism. Uniquely they are permitted to visit soldiers and airmen/women in their accommodation, work and recreation areas. This is done with a view to befriending them and introducing them to the Lord Jesus Christ through His Word the Bible.

Who are the Scripture Readers and what is their purpose?

They are all believing Christians and ex-Forces who feel a personal calling to the work, with the aim that the serving personnel of the British Army and Royal Air Force all hear the gospel.

When and how did it start?

Around 1818 there was a certain Sergeant Rudd with the Royal Artillery at Woolwich. He put a card in the garrison guardroom offering to loan a bible to anyone who wished to have it. However, this had been done without permission and Rudd was reprimanded by his CO (commanding officer). But one Captain Maitland heard about it. He was so encouraged by what Rudd had done that he had Bibles placed around the garrison at his own expense. This was also disapproved of by the CO and the Bibles were removed. However, Captain Maitland's father was a high-ranking officer and after he intervened, a wagonload of Bibles was sent to Woolwich to be placed in every guardroom and the hospital. This event likely influenced those in authority about the spiritual welfare of soldiers.

In 1825, King's Regulations authorised, at public expense, the issue of a Bible and Prayer Book to all soldiers who desired to have them.

By 1828 a 'Soldiers' Friend Society' had been established and in 1838 it was renamed to include 'Scripture Readers' in the title. In 1886 the Soldiers' Christian Association began a similar spiritual welfare role and in 1930 all were grouped into one association.

An account from World War 2

Frederick Howe was a soldier during WW1 and became a Scripture Reader in 1935, posted to the Middle East to serve in Egypt and then Crete, where he faithfully shared the Gospel with the troops. He was involved in military action, about which he wrote...

"...[we were] machine-gunned and bombed in the valleys. Bombed and machine-gunned in hospital, an amazing dash across the island with wounded men. Caught again on the mountains, a dash to the beach with the wounded...tracts in German given to wounded Nazi prisoners. God was in it all. Never once did one lose the sense of the presence of the Saviour. "Lo, I am with you always." This is what I call Army Scripture Readers' work. God has richly blessed the work. All goes well. I am, sir, very sincerely yours, In His Love and Happy Service."

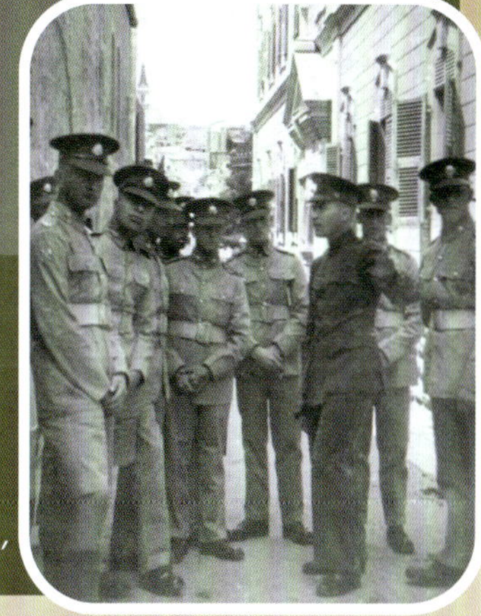

He was part of the evacuation from Crete and returned to Egypt where he was involved in a serious motor accident. He was then put on a ship home in July 1942—the SS Laconia, which was attacked and sunk by a U-boat off the coast of Africa. He became the only Scripture Reader to die in military action during the war. SASRA wrote to their supporters to inform them of his death: *'We thank God for having loaned to the Association such a one who was ever found about his Master's business.'*

What does SASRA do now?

Since 1950, the organisation has been known as SASRA and continues the work of mission to the serving personnel of the British Army and the Royal Air Force. It served alongside soldiers abroad in both World Wars and is ready to go with serving personnel on overseas deployments. Scripture Readers lead worship and Bible studies, and provide pastoral care, support and instruction.

From police cell to Bible study leader!

One example of how SASRA helps today is the story of a young man 'John,' who had been a drug dealer. When banged up in a police cell, he felt so in need of help that he prayed for the first time. He joined the Army, went to church and started reading his Bible.

At this point a SASRA Scripture Reader came alongside him and they studied Matthew, Romans and Acts. He was teased a lot for his new faith, but SASRA was there to encourage and support him. He came to believe in the Lord Jesus Christ as his saviour and was baptised in 2022. He joined a church and became a Bible study leader himself.

Two aspects of SASRA's work today: (left) Bible distribution, these are New Testaments, Psalms & Proverbs; (right) holding Bible studies

F-15E Strike Eagle jet fighter-bomber of the US Air Force being refuelled

90227
NO STEP
NO STEP

NUCLEAR WEAPONS

Splitting the atom: harnessing nature's power to make super-bombs

DID YOU KNOW?
The term 'Armageddon' comes from Revelation 16:16 where it is said to be the location of the last ever battle

Ushering in Armageddon or keeping the peace?

The atomic bomb is arguably the most controversial item ever invented. It is a fearsome weapon of almost unimaginable destruction which harnesses the power of nature by splitting atoms of radioactive material like uranium and plutonium. First developed during WW2 in a top secret operation called the Manhattan Project which employed 130,000 people, it was dropped on two Japanese cities in August 1945 causing widespread devastation. Fierce arguments followed, with its supporters saying that it forced Japan to surrender and thereby saved the lives of many soldiers on both sides who would have been killed if US troops had invaded Japan, outweighing the number of Japanese killed and injured by the bombs. But others said that targeting civilians in cities that weren't important for the war effort was cruel and the US were determined to demonstrate their immense power to frighten and control other countries.

After WW2, the US and some Western nations were in a race with the Soviet Union to develop bigger and better nuclear weapons, supposedly to act as a deterrent to stop the other side starting another war. It made people really fearful as they were worried that the world would be destroyed by nuclear war, and this was especially true during the Cuban Missile Crisis, when in 1962 the Soviets moved nuclear missiles close to the US. In 1968, a new treaty was agreed where nations would limit stockpiles of nuclear weapons. It is still in force today.

A bomb casing similar to the atomic bomb dropped on Nagasaki, Japan

LEARNING POINT

A few tonnes of radioactive material contains enough energy to flatten a city like London. However, the bomb only releases a small fraction of the total energy contained in that material. Imagine how much energy is stored in all the atoms throughout the whole universe! Where did all that energy come from? The Bible tells us that Jesus made the world (John 1:3) and all power is given unto Him (Matthew 28:18). He sustains the universe by the 'Word of His power' (Hebrews 1:3). At the end of time, when Jesus comes again, the universe will melt with intense heat when every atom will be dissolved. Surely this helps us consider God's immense power. We should be humbled!

THE BIBLE SAYS . . .
'The heavens being on fire shall be dissolved, and the elements shall melt with fervent heat.' (2 Peter 3:12)

DID YOU KNOW?

The most powerful nuclear weapon ever detonated, developed by the Soviet Union, was 1,500 times more powerful than **both** bombs dropped on Japan in 1945. The blast wave circled the Earth 3 times and the mushroom cloud was 8 times taller than Mt. Everest

(above) Mushroom cloud from the 2nd nuclear bomb dropped on Japan: Nagasaki, 9 Aug 1945

(above right) The fireball from a test explosion of a small artillery-fired weapon, Nevada, USA, April 1953; note the trees bottom left for scale

(right) Devastation of Hiroshima, Japan, after the first atomic bomb drop, 6 August 1945

'Subs'—Ships that can 'sail' under the sea

DID YOU KNOW?
The German name 'U-boat' comes from 'Unterseeboot' meaning 'under sea boat', much like the English 'sub' (below) 'marine' (sea)

Menace of the Deep

Getting close to your enemy without being seen is an advantage in any situation, but especially so at sea when there are no trees or hills to hide behind! Submarines as a concept have been around for a few centuries. Early inventors hoped they could be used to sail underwater to sneak right up to an enemy ship, at which point men would leave the 'sub' and plant explosives.

In the First World War submarines came into their own as a powerful weapon. The invention of diesel engines, batteries and electric motors gave them effective propulsion on the surface and underwater, and periscopes helped to spot enemy shipping whilst remaining submerged. Until the advent of missiles, the main weapon fired by submarines was the torpedo—a self-propelled machine with an explosive warhead. Some early subs were equipped with a waterproof hangar housing a seaplane which could be launched and flown ahead of the fleet to locate the enemy.

During the 1940s, most submarines could only stay under the water about 24 hours, though some could manage 3 days at a push. Modern nuclear-powered subs can sail underwater all the way around the world, and stay hidden for a year, until such time they need to be called into action.

Space is very limited on a submarine and being a submariner is no place for the claustrophobic (*fear of confined spaces*). Lack of windows and daylight must give the feeling of being entombed in a metal coffin deep under the waves—not for the faint-hearted. At least modern subs have air conditioning, unlike old wartime models where the air became pungent and stale.

LEARNING POINT

Until the invention of the modern submarine, it was Jonah who had been under the sea for longer than anyone else—in the belly of a whale, fish or sea creature which God had prepared specially to swallow him and save him from drowning. What a miserable experience it must have been in pitch blackness, wrapped in seaweed (Jonah 2:5)! Jonah said it was like being in the 'belly of hell.' Jesus said to the Jews that Jonah's horrible experience was a sign or prophecy to them—that as Jonah was 'buried' in the sea and then came out of it, so Christ would have to die and go into the grave, before He would be raised again to life. The Jewish rulers did not believe Him, and many do not even today. But do you and I believe that Jesus rose from the dead?

THE BIBLE SAYS ...
'For as *Jonah* was three days and three nights in the whale's belly; so shall the Son of man be three days and three nights in the heart of the earth.' (Matthew 12:40)

above) USS Los Angeles nuclear-powered sub; (above right) a modern orpedo which can listen for a ship's propellers and steer itself to the target; below) sleeping quarters on the USS Skate, 1958; (right) A Norwegian sub urfaces off the coast of Iceland; (below right) Royal Navy sub HMS M2 in ervice 1918-1932 with its seaplane being launched from a catapult

(above) USS Key West sailing at periscope depth in the blue waters of Hawaii, 2004

(below) An unarmed Trident II missile is launched from the submerged submarine USS Maine off the coast of San Diego, 2020. The Trident can carry a nuclear warhead

(inset right) The periscope of HMS Talent during a training exercise in Scotland, 2009

Astute class nuclear-powered sub of the Royal Navy undergoing sea trials in 2012

STEALTH

Making combat aircraft 'invisible'

Surprise, surprise!

Staying unnoticed helps combat aircraft to fulfil their mission safely. The objective is to avoid drawing attention to your presence. Here are some ways combat aircraft do this:

HIDDEN FROM SIGHT

Flying low behind hills and trees to avoid being spotted by eye or radar. Night flying with/without night vision goggles.

LOW OBSERVABILITY

Match the colour of the surroundings, applying a matt (not shiny) paint. Camouflage pattern to make it harder to spot.

LOW NOISE

Design of rotor blades and engines to reduce noise. Engine exhausts located on top of the plane, not at the back.

LOW HEAT

Disperse the engine exhausts to reduce the 'heat signature', to improve chances of evading heat-seeking missiles.

LOW RADAR SIGNATURE

Ensuring the shape of a plane does not return radar waves back to the enemy radar. Use of radar absorbent material.

STAND OFF (AT A DISTANCE)

Firing 'beyond visual range' (BVR) long range missiles to remain out of harm's way (up to 120 miles / 200km away).

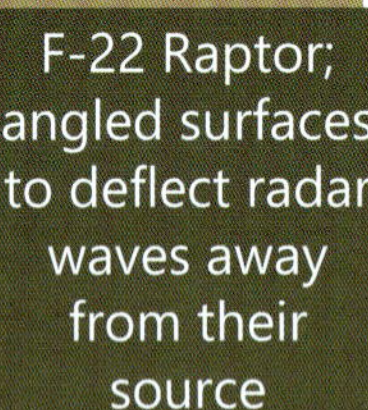

F-22 Raptor; angled surfaces to deflect radar waves away from their source

AH-64 Apache Longbow; Weapon aiming sensors in rotor mount to allow it to hide behind trees and peer over the top

Three RAF Typhoons painted in low visibility grey to blend in at high altitudes

F-14 Tomcat firing a Phoenix long range missile weighing about 1,000lb / 450kg

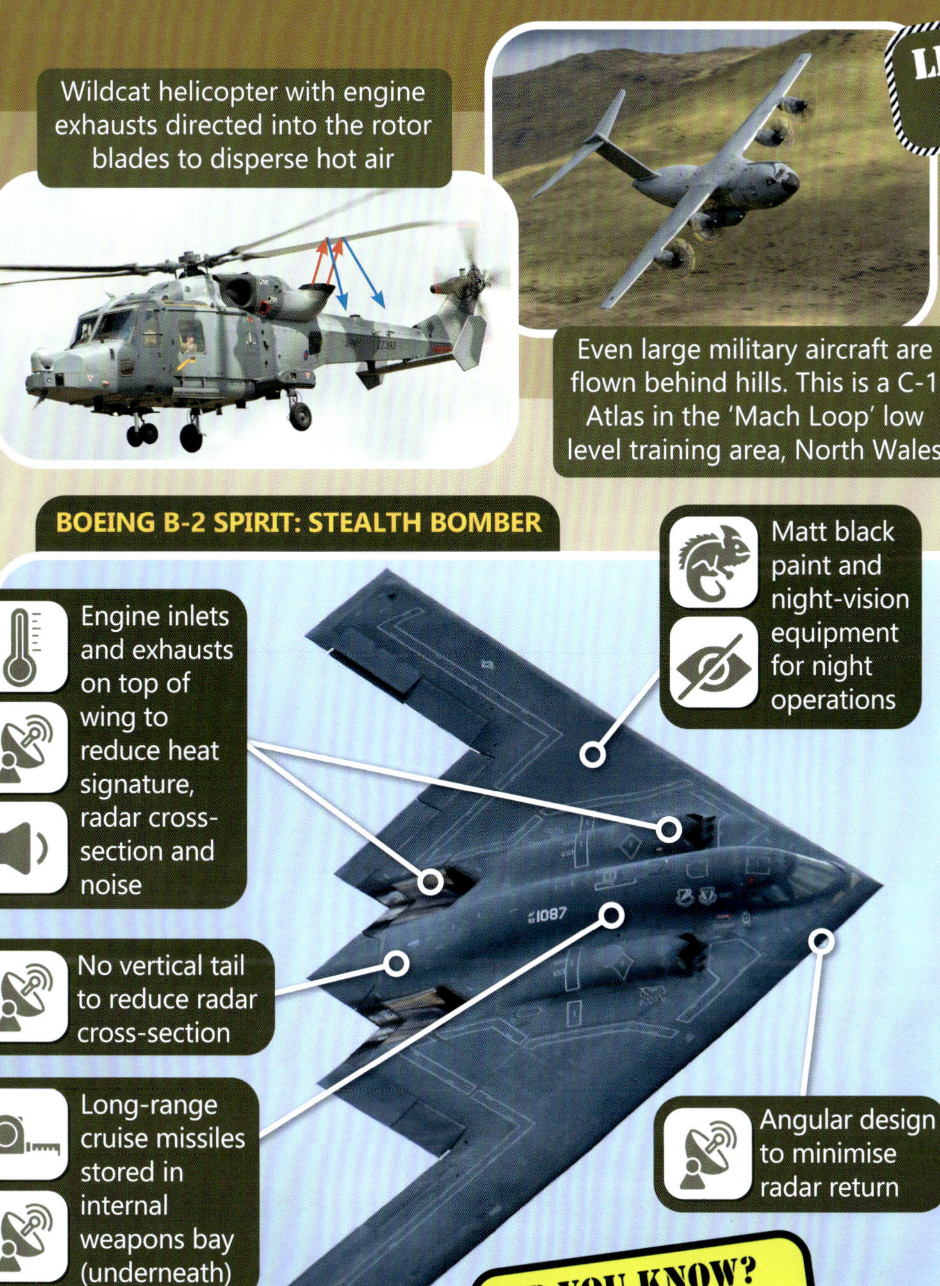

Wildcat helicopter with engine exhausts directed into the rotor blades to disperse hot air

Even large military aircraft are flown behind hills. This is a C-1 Atlas in the 'Mach Loop' low level training area, North Wales

BOEING B-2 SPIRIT: STEALTH BOMBER

LEARNING POINT

Why did Boeing call the B-2 the 'Spirit'? The word spirit is often used to describe a life without a body, such as a ghost (as some think). In other words, something unseen, and yet with life and power. The B-2 is designed to drop bombs or fire missiles (so it is a powerful weapon) but to do so stealthily (without being seen or heard).

God is one God, but a Trinity of three persons—God the Father, God the Son and God the Holy **Spirit**. The Holy Spirit works powerfully yet silently in the hearts of men and women to convince them they are sinners and show them God the Father's love in sending Jesus as Saviour. The Holy Spirit does not draw attention to Himself. He works without being seen, but His work makes all the difference!

DID YOU KNOW?

The B-2 is the most expensive plane ever made ($737 million each)

THE BIBLE SAYS . . .

The Holy Spirit's work is like a wind blowing in the heart; no-one knows where it comes from or where it goes to. The wind cannot be seen, but we can see and know its effects. Read what Jesus said in John 3:5-8.

(above) F-22 Raptor stealthy jet fighter tumbling through the air, firing flares used to decoy heat-seeking missiles, at a US airshow, 2024; (opposite page) the F-35B which can hover, replacing the BAe Harrier 'jump jet' in the RAF and US Marine Corps; (right) stealth technology is being applied to navy ships; here is a US ship and a Singapore Navy frigate the RSS Steadfast ('70')

DEPLOYMENT

Leaving 'base' to go overseas

A joyful reunion returning from deployment

Wish you were here?

Armed forces will sometimes go overseas on deployment. This is to temporarily relocate away from their home base(s) to where they are needed. This may be to keep the peace, deter an aggressor, take part in active operations (warfare) or for training. A key benefit is the opportunity to use weapons and prove tactics in a wide variety of climates like jungles, deserts and icy regions. Peacetime deployments can last from a few weeks to a year. In a navy they may last 12-18 months if they are sent to patrol international waters when political tensions are running high between countries and there is a fear that war may break out. On returning home, family reunions can be emotional events.

LEARNING POINT

Wherever personnel go on overseas deployment—no matter which country, climate or local culture—they must never lose sight of why they are there and who they serve. Likewise, when those who love Jesus are spending time 'in the world', perhaps at school, university or work, they must remember whose they are and who they serve (Acts 27:23). A Christian's real home is not here on Earth but in Heaven where Jesus is (John 15:19, Philippians 3:20, Hebrews 13:14). Nevertheless, day by day, God wants them just where they are, here on the Earth. They must not forget their mission which is to do the will of God, not getting distracted (2 Timothy 2:4). What is God's will? It is to believe completely on Jesus; to love reading His Word; to meet at church or chapel to worship Him and encourage others; to do good to all and love one another; and, as we can, to be a witness for Jesus.

Christians are called 'strangers and pilgrims' in a strange land, like Abraham was when he was in the Promised Land (Hebrews 11:13). God had told him to go and live there in a tent, moving from place to place. Yet Abraham never forgot that he was there because God had sent him. Moses fled his home in Egypt and spent 40 years in Midian away from everyone he knew, often out in the desert as a shepherd (Exodus 2:22, 3:1). He never forgot his people back in Egypt.

Do you follow Jesus? If so, will you serve Him faithfully wherever you are?

THE BIBLE SAYS . . .

'As for me and my *household*, we will serve the LORD.' (Joshua 24:15)

What does Peter say to believers in 1 Peter 2:11-12?

(left, above) British commandos on winter deployment in Norway

(right, top to bottom) Australian soldiers practice a jungle river crossing, Brunei; 3rd Battalion, the Parachute Regiment on the Kenyan savannah; US Marine at the Jungle Warfare Training Centre, Japan

DID YOU KNOW?

In 2023, Royal Marines went to the Caribbean, Sudan, the Persian Gulf, West African Coast, Kenya, South Korea, Australia, Sweden, Estonia, Finland, the Mediterranean and California

ON THE FRONT LINE

Away from comforts and where danger is all around

DID YOU KNOW?
74,000 British soldiers suffered from Trench Foot in WW1

First World War

No bed, no bathroom

Being on the front line, where the battle is fought, is by its nature a harsh and often miserable experience, even when not engaged in the fighting. Although troops do their best to make themselves comfortable, they have to sleep in the open or tents and wash in whatever water is available. Food may be scarce and communication with home unlikely.

The conditions suffered by men in the trenches of WW1, including Trench Foot, are described by Frank Boorman from Kent, who was a Christian in the British Army. He wrote:

"Nobody in England can imagine what the troops in the trenches have to endure in mud and water up to their knees and often to their waist for 48 hours at a stretch. The authorities try to [help], providing pumps, waterproof boxes and tubs for the men to stand in ... It is a sight to see the poor men after leaving the trenches caked in mud and hobbling like old men. Their feet swell to an incredible size and turn blue, and boots and socks of many have to be cut off." [January 1915]

(top) The horrendous conditions are shown in WW1 trenches in Flanders, Belgium, 1918; at least these men were not being shot at, and it wasn't dark and raining...

(above) A filthy British soldier keeps watch as two comrades nap

LEARNING POINT

There are countless war stories where soldiers have endured terrible suffering. The Apostle Paul himself had suffered so much, being beaten and nearly stoned to death, as he travelled around to spread the Gospel. When he wrote to his young friend Timothy, he encouraged him and told him to bear with all the difficulties which he would have in being a follower of Jesus, in the same way that a soldier has to cope in terrible conditions. All believers need to look to Jesus, praying for strength to endure and not complain, day by day (1 Corinthians 10:9-10).

THE BIBLE SAYS . . .

'I endure all things for the elect's sakes, that they may also obtain the salvation which is in Christ Jesus.' (2 Timothy 2:10)

'Endure hardness, as a good soldier of Jesus Christ.' (2 Timothy 2:3)

(top left) Keeping watch from a dug-out with sandbags; (top right) US Marines coming back from the front lines, Saipan, Pacific Ocean, 1944; (right) Soldiers from 9 Parachute Regiment patrol in a Jackal armoured vehicle in Helmand Province, Afghanistan, 2011; patrols have been at risk from IEDs (Improvised Explosive Devices, i.e. roadside bombs)

FEEDING THE TROOPS

Mass catering 'in the field'

No food = no energy = no victory

'An army marches on its stomach' is a well-known saying often attributed to Napoleon Bonaparte (1769-1821), the master military French leader who conquered all of continental Europe. He understood that hungry soldiers will become weakened in battle and lose focus, or struggle if required to march quickly to the battle front. Hunger is a survival instinct telling our bodies to ensure we get food as soon we can. It begins as a distraction, which then grows into gnawing pain and, if not addressed, leads to illness and death. Keeping an army fed should be a priority.

THEN and NOW

As an army moves about, it is vital that chefs, food and temporary cooking facilities—called field kitchens—are moved close to where the soldiers are staying or fighting.

(far left) A woman of the Queen Mary's Auxiliary Army Corps preparing dinner in Rouen, France 1918; (left) Food being served in a modern British Army field kitchen

LEARNING POINT

Christians should follow the example of the Lord Jesus who gave thanks to His Heavenly Father when He ate a meal (Mark 8:6). Do not be unthankful or take your food for granted—it is a blessing!

The Bible tells us that Christians, who are in the fight of faith (1 Timothy 6:12), need to eat *spiritual food* every day to stay strong. What is this spiritual food? The Bible says it is these three things:

THE BIBLE SAYS . . .

'Give us this day our daily bread.' (Matthew 6:11)

'I am the living bread which came down from heaven: if any man eat of this bread, he shall live for ever.' (John 6:51)

1. KNOWING GOD'S WORD

By reading the Bible, Christians are strengthened to continue because they are reminded of Jesus' love to them and their hope of Heaven. (Read John 6:63)

2. DOING GOD'S WILL

Jesus said that doing His Father's will was His food (John 4:34). That meant that it was His focus, what kept Him going, like food does for our bodies.

3. JESUS HIMSELF!

Jesus says of Himself that He is bread (quote above). To sit at His feet and learn from Him is the 'one thing needful.' (Luke 10:42)

DID YOU KNOW?
An average man needs 2,500 calories of food a day. Soldiers on active service need about 3-4,000 rising to 6,000 cals/day in combat

(above) US Marines learn how to forage (find) and cook their food on training in Hawaii in 2022; (below left) A kitchen on a Vanguard-class nuclear-powered submarine of the Royal Navy; (below right) A US Army field kitchen.

MILITARY MUSIC

Musical instruments to communicate with and rally the troops

DID YOU KNOW?
The first military 'musical' instrument named in the Bible is a shofar (ram's horn)

Advance to the beat of the drum

The playing of musical instruments has for thousands of years been an important part of warfare, certainly since the time when the Israelites came out of Egypt (Numbers 10:9) in about 1500 BC. Why was this? In days gone by with no radios or telephones, communicating with a vast army of soldiers wasn't easy, so sounding short or long blasts on a horn, which could be heard a distance away and above the noise of battle, was a good way to get attention and issue instructions.

The Greeks and Romans also used to play music in battle as they recounted previous victories, because it gave the troops courage to continue. However, it was the Crusades in the 12th and 13th centuries that gave rise to the modern military tradition of marching bands, as the European soldiers saw how the Saracens played a variety of instruments in battle including drums, which distressed the Crusaders' horses whilst encouraging the Saracen soldiers. From that time onwards, military music, as we know it today, took shape. Snare drums became especially important as the steady beat raised morale amongst the troops and disheartened the enemy.

Nowadays, military bands are only used for special events, as modern technology and tactics have dramatically changed the battlefield.

A trumpeter of the US Marine Corps at a funeral at the National Cemetery, Arlington

LEARNING POINT

In ancient times, when a horn or trumpet was blown to sound an alert, gathering the fighting men to the battle, how important it was that the sound should be clear so there was no misunderstanding. Correctly hearing the call to battle was a matter of life and death. Likewise, when we are talking about something important, we should use simple and clear language so we can be easily understood. The Apostle Paul said that Christian leaders, and anyone who wants to encourage other Christians, should use plain speech. The Good News of salvation in Jesus Christ, and the Bible's message to those who believe, is too important to be misunderstood!

THE BIBLE SAYS...
'For if the trumpet give an uncertain sound, who shall prepare himself to the battle?' (1 Corinthians 14:8)

Drum Horse Major Atlas, with kettle drums, leading the Mounted Band of the Household Cavalry at King Charles III's coronation

This famous hymn was written for Sunday School children to sing, to encourage them as they walked up the hill from Horbury Bridge to Horbury Parish church, a mile from my home.

ONWARD CHRISTIAN SOLDIERS

Onward, Christian soldiers, marching as to war,
With the cross of Jesus going on before!
Christ, the royal Master, leads against the foe;
Forward into battle, see his banner go!

At the sign of triumph Satan's host doth flee;
On, then, Christian soldiers, on to victory!
Hell's foundations quiver at the shout of praise;
Brothers, lift your voices, loud your anthems raise!

Like a mighty army moves the church of God;
Brothers, we are treading where the saints have
We are not divided; all one body we, [trod;
One in hope and doctrine, one in charity.

Onward, then, ye people, join our happy throng,
Blend with ours your voices in the triumph song;
Glory, laud, and honour, unto Christ the King;
This thro' countless ages men and angels sing!

(Mr) Sabine Baring-Gould 1834-1924

The Band of the Irish Guards, led by their mascot, an Irish wolfhound, at the Queen's birthday parade

COMBAT

Fighting on the battlefield

In the heat of battle

When a military force engages in fighting, it is time to put their training into practice. But even advanced training cannot fully prepare soldiers for the horror of war. It is common for veterans who have fought in combat to refuse to talk about the things they went through. To see friends being shot, or hearing them scream when their limbs are blown off, can leave a man affected for the rest of his life. Or it may be the guilt of killing or maiming someone, causing nightmares afterwards.

In WW1, which was the first large scale intense war with non-stop bombardment and modern weapons, some men were so affected by the constant, deafening noise of explosions, and of the horror around them, that they went crazy, sobbed uncontrollably, couldn't sleep, wandered off or deserted. It was known as "shell shock" and is now called PTSD (Post-Traumatic Stress Disorder).

It has been said that, ahead of going into battle, 'anyone who says he isn't afraid is lying.' The anxiety waiting to attack can be so strong that soldiers vomit. Knowing all these things and pressing forward an attack against the enemy takes real courage.

LEARNING POINT

When the Israelites were told by God to go into the Promised Land and fight those who lived there, they were very afraid. They were not trained, well-equipped soldiers. They faced grim hand-to-hand combat. God spoke kindly to them and said that they should not be afraid because He was fighting with them in the battle. Their success was not in their own ability but in God's who would protect them (Joshua 1:9).

Christians in battle have similarly drawn comfort from knowing God is with them and in control, and nothing can separate them from His love, whether they live or die (Romans 8:35). As a hymn by John Ryland beautifully puts it, 'Not a single *shot* can hit, *until* the God of love sees fit.'

It is a blessing if we live in a time of peace. But the spiritual battle rages on, as Satan seeks to cause misery to everyone in the world, especially to those who believe in Jesus. Satan can tempt Christians to desert—saying to them that life would be easier and more comfortable if they gave up their faith. He says, "The Bible isn't true, God is lying" or "God loves sinners, but not someone as bad as you!" But God is fighting for His people against Satan and He will win at last. It is God who keeps them safe (Psalm 28:7; Isaiah 26:3-4). Where is your trust, and mine?

THE BIBLE SAYS . . .

'Approach ... unto battle against your enemies: let not your hearts faint, fear not, and do not tremble ... for the LORD your God is he that *goes* with you, to fight for you against your enemies, to save you.' (Deuteronomy 20:3-4)

'The horse is prepared for the day of battle: but safety is of the LORD.' (Proverbs 21:31)

DID YOU KNOW?
At the Battle of the Somme (1916) as many as 40% of British casualties were shell-shocked

(above) US 1st and 16th Infantry wade from a landing craft onto Omaha beach, Normandy, 6 June 1944 (D-Day); (bottom left) UH-1H Hueys drop off South Vietnamese troops in the Vietnam War, 1970; (bottom right) A Paratrooper takes cover after throwing a grenade at a Taliban position, Afghanistan, 2008

AGAINST THE ODDS

Some battles which seemed to be hopeless, but weren't

Outnumbered

There have been battles in history where one side seemed so outnumbered or weak that defeat would be certain, but they won. The Bible contains many accounts of battles and sieges won by the 'underdog,' through God's help (Have a go at the quiz on **page 57**). Here are two accounts in recent British history where the odds seemed overwhelming.

DID YOU KNOW?
King George VI called 7 National Days of Prayer in WW2

The Battle of Britain, 1940

When Adolf Hitler invaded and then conquered Holland, Belgium and France in 1940, the British Army was pushed out of Europe in such a hurry that they had to be evacuated from Dunkirk, France, by fishing boats and other small ships, and they had to abandon most of their equipment on the beach. Although bringing the Army back safely was rightly seen as a great miracle in answer to a National Day of Prayer on 27th March, Britain was left without an effective army and open to invasion. The Nazis seemed invincible and Britain was alone with a difficult choice—ask for a peace deal with Hitler, or fight on. The British government decided to fight on despite the British Army being so weak, and Germany's air force, the Luftwaffe, having 3 times as many planes as the RAF.

Pilots of 303 (Polish) Squadron; some of the 3,000 RAF airmen called "the Few"

Hitler ordered the Luftwaffe to quickly destroy the RAF so he could safely get his troops across the English Channel before the bad weather later in the year. They launched intense air raids from June to September, sending hundreds of bombers and fighters in wave after wave. The RAF had to scramble to intercept them day after day, and exhaustion and lack of fresh pilots was a major problem. But incredibly, the RAF held out and, after another National Day of Prayer on 9th September, the Germans gave up.

A shot down Bf109 with bullet holes

"Never in the field of human conflict was so much owed by so many to so few."
Sir Winston Churchill, August 1940

Siege of the island of Malta, 1940-1942

In WW2, both sides were fighting for control of the Mediterranean Sea and North Africa. The Nazi General Rommel said that "without Malta the Axis [Germans and her allies] will end by losing control of North Africa." To the Axis it was critical to capture it. They resolved to bomb Malta and cut off shipping to starve the island into surrender. They bombed an average of four times a day for two and a half years. In 1942, the capital city Valetta became the most bombed place on Earth.

The ruins of Valetta, April 1942

"It may be that hard times lay ahead of us, but I know that however hard they be ... with God's help we will maintain the security of this fortress. I call on all officers and other ranks humbly to seek God's help, and then in reliance on Him to do their duty unflinchingly."

Sir William Dobbie

The island forces were under the command of a devout British Christian, Sir William Dobbie. The Commander-in-Chief of the Mediterranean Fleet said of Dobbie, "His profound [Protestant] faith in the justice of our cause made a great impression on the religious [Catholic] Maltese. The complete and calm faith shown in the broadcasts he made nearly every evening contributed immensely towards keeping up the morale of the people."

DID YOU KNOW?
In just two months there were 500 air raids on Malta

The poor island had been left with no air force to protect it, but a number of outdated Gloster Sea Gladiator biplanes were found in bits. Mechanics assembled them and generally kept three airworthy. They took to the skies to attack the invading bombers although they were no match for the invaders. They were later nicknamed Faith, Hope and Charity, from Paul's words in 1 Corinthians 13:13. Spitfires were sent to defend the island and, in late 1942, the Germans quit the siege.

Gloster Gladiator

LEARNING POINT

Does life seem overwhelming? Does it look as though evil is winning when you look around, and hear the news, and struggle with sin in your own life? Satan and his demons are powerful. What can you do, or I? But God is great. He can use the weak and the few to change the lives of others for good, especially in salvation (1 Corinthians 1:27).

THE BIBLE SAYS . . .
'There is no *limit* to the LORD to save by many or by few.' (1 Samuel 14:6)

CODE BREAKING

Coding and decoding secret messages

DID YOU KNOW?

A code replaces entire words or phrases whereas a cipher replaces individual letters. We often use the word 'code' when we mean 'cipher'

Hidden meaning

Any military force which knows exactly what the enemy will do next has a huge tactical advantage. It may enable forces to be strengthened where needed, or prevent an attack (see 2 Kings 6:8-12). It is therefore important for any messages being sent electronically or by paper, radio or telephone to be **coded** so that they can only be read by those who also have the same code as you. If those messages are intercepted, they won't make sense, unless the code or cipher is known.

(above) The German 'Enigma' machine used in WW2 was a work of genius. If any letter, say 'T', was pressed 100 times, it would return any other letter of the alphabet in a seeming random order. There were literally billions of ways a message could be coded. It was so secure that the Germans thought it unbreakable, but mathematicians and other academics at Bletchley Park, near London, found how to crack the codes once an Enigma machine and a German code book had been captured. Some think this was the most important victory by the Allies in the war.

LEARNING POINT

Jesus spoke using parables so that some of His hearers, like the self-important rulers of His day would not understand Him; it was like a coded message. Jesus did not come to save the proud who thought they had no need of forgiveness. He came for poor and needy sinners; they understood His message (Matthew 13:10-11) and willingly received it!

THE BIBLE SAYS . . .

'I [Jesus] came not to call the righteous, but sinners to repentance.' (Luke 5:32)

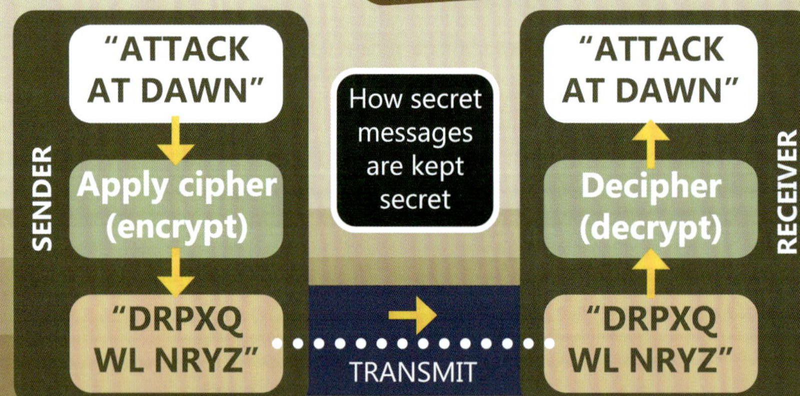

Bible challenge

"AGAINST THE ODDS" CODE-BREAKING QUIZ

Answers: page 76

Here are 9 times in the Bible when the Lord's people were given victory or kept safe, when it looked as though the situation was impossible. Look up each Bible passage given and work out which are the right answers from the ones provided. You will need to identify:

- » WHO was the person that God used to bring the victory about;
- » HOW did God bring it about - pick an answer from the white boxes below the table
- » Optional: who were the ENEMY - find the answer in the Bible.

Note that the name of the person who God used (the "Who") has been scrambled using a code. Each letter has been replaced with the one before it in the alphabet. So for example, LNRDR would be decoded as MOSES as the next letter in the alphabet after 'L' is 'M' and so on (L goes to M, N goes to O, R goes to S, D goes to E, R goes to S).

Use a pen and paper!

CODED	A	B	C	D	E	F	G	H	I	J	K	L	M	N	O	P	Q	R	S	T	U	V	W	X	Y	Z
DECODED	B	C	D	E	F	G	H	I	J	K	L	M	N	O	P	Q	R	S	T	U	V	W	X	Y	Z	A

BIBLE REF	WHO (CODED)	WHO? (DECODED)	HOW?	ENEMY?
1) Exodus 14	LNRDR	MOSES	Strong wind	Pharaoh & army
2) Judges 4-5 (5:21)	CDANQZG			
3) Judges 7	FHCDNM			
4) Judges 15	RZLRNM			
5) 1 Samuel 13-14	INMZSGZM			
6) 1 Samuel 17	CZUHC			
7) 2 Kings 6:8-23	DKHRGZ			
8) 2 Kings 7	DKHRGZ			
9) Isaiah 37	HRZHZG			

Pick an answer from these boxes for 'HOW?'

- Enemy panic
- Imagining noise
- Blindness
- Courage and skill
- Prophecy & courage
- Angel of the LORD
- Supernatural strength
- River flooding

DID YOU KNOW?
Secret codes were vital for the work of SOE (see next page)

SABOTAGE!
Undercover agents deceiving and destroying

Friend or foe?

A spy is someone who gathers information ('intelligence') about the opposition, usually by entering enemy territory disguised to avoid being discovered. Sending spies has long been a part of warfare (Genesis 42:9, Joshua 2:1). At times, these spies have become infiltrators, that is, they take on a whole character, language and personality of someone and work their way into the military or other organisation in order to cause trouble and confusion, hampering the enemy's efforts. Another tactic may be to pretend to be an ordinary citizen, but in secret carry out acts of sabotage, often targeting the transport and communication networks—such as cutting telephone wires, destroying railway lines and blowing up bridges. What is the purpose of sabotage? It is to weaken the enemy from within, where they are not expecting it.

Notable sabotage in recent history includes Germans destroying warehouses and ships in New York in WW1. Also, the work of the French, Polish and Norwegian Resistance movements during WW2 was significant. Britain set up an organisation called Special Operations Executive (SOE) to send the Resistance supplies and drop in secret agents. They used Lysander aircraft for this, as they could land and take off from unprepared fields at night, to avoid being seen.

DID YOU KNOW?
'Sabotage' is derived from a French word meaning to bungle, botch or wreck

WHAT IS SABOTAGE?
If You See Someone
Deliberately BREAKING TOOLS or RUINING MACHINES–
Failing to do a FULL DAY'S WORK–
Knowingly PRODUCING or PASSING INFERIOR MATERIAL–
Intentionally WASTING TIME or MATERIALS–
Thoughtlessly BLABBING JOB SECRETS to outsiders–
Encouraging DISHONESTY, DISLOYALTY or DISHONOR–
Or doing anything fishy
TO DELAY OUR WAR PRODUCTION
Smash these scurvy tricks to make America helpless!
–BECAUSE–
SABOTAGE IS TREASON!

A US poster informing workers what to look out for to spot sabotage at work, 1942-43

LEARNING POINT

Deceiving the enemy is a legitimate wartime tactic even approved of by God Himself (Joshua 8:2, also see Judges 7:19-22, 2 Kings 7:5-7 and James 2:25). Christians do, however, need to be aware that Satan regularly uses deception as a tactic. He is the father of lies (John 8:44) and he wants nothing more than the destruction of the Church as that is where Jesus' name is preached (Revelation 12:17). Satan works hard to infiltrate churches with false teachers who appear good to start with, but in the end they turn people away from trusting in the person and work of Christ (2 Corinthians 11:13-14). How important is faith in Jesus! (1 Peter 5:8-9)

THE BIBLE SAYS . . .

'Beware of false prophets, which come to you in sheep's clothing, but inwardly they are *ravenous* wolves.' (Matthew 7:15)

'Many deceivers are entered into the world, who confess not that Jesus Christ is come in the flesh.' (2 John 1:7) [Also read Jude 1:4]

(left, above left) Civilians in Occupied France became members of the French Resistance to make life as difficult as possible for the Nazi forces; (above right) Destruction of a railway bridge in Visegrad by Chetniks of the former Yugoslavian Army, 1943; (below) Westland Lysander Mk.III painted in black for night operations; it could fly as slow as 65mph/104kph and carry 3 passengers.

SPECIAL FORCES

Highly-trained soldiers operating in enemy territory

SPECIAL AIR SERVICE REGIMENT

WHO DARES WINS

Experts in sudden destruction

Battles have historically been fought with large armies, using weight of numbers to beat the opposing side. Down through the ages, armies have often had groups of highly-trained elite soldiers, but it was not until the Second World War when covert (secret) operations became a regular part of modern warfare with the inception of the British SAS.

Whereas a large army can be easily spotted and requires significant logistical support (food, fuel, ammunition etc.), a small group of commandos can move quickly to destroy high-value and well-defended targets without warning. Although the SAS's first mission was a disaster, the second was a resounding success, and now all major military powers have their own Special Forces. The SAS is especially remembered for ending the siege of the Iranian Embassy in London in 1980, live on TV.

DID YOU KNOW?

The Special Air Service (SAS), whose motto is 'Who Dares Wins,' was the brainchild of David Stirling. It was first operational in 1941 in North Africa against the Germans.

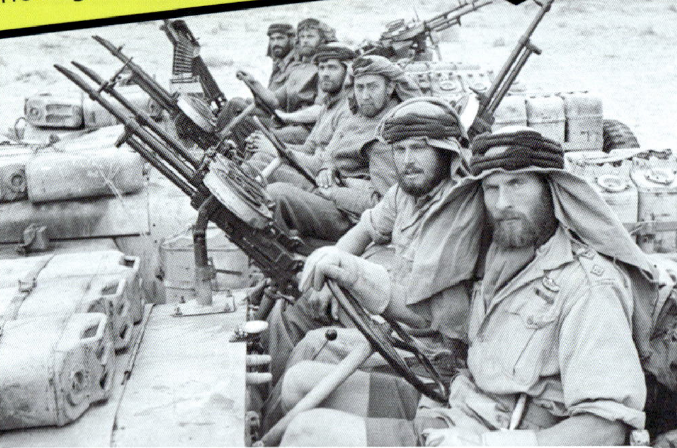

Men of the SAS in their Jeeps, returning from a 3 month patrol, North Africa, 1943. Notice the large amount of fuel and water for desert operations

LEARNING POINT

Special forces are often successful because they use the element of surprise. They get in and get out as quickly as possible, before they are found. Many operations are at night because it is easier to stay hidden under the cover of darkness. The Bible tells us that many will be caught out at the end of time when the Lord Jesus Christ will come back to Earth ('the day of the Lord'). When He appears, it will be sudden and unexpected. Jesus said that no-one knows the day or time when He will come again. To those who believe the Bible though, it will not be a complete shock. But to everyone else, it will come with destruction and without warning, and then it will be too late.

THE BIBLE SAYS . . .

The day of the Lord *comes* as a thief in the night. For when they shall say, Peace and safety; then sudden destruction *comes* upon them... and they shall not escape..' (1 Thessalonians 5:2-3)

(above) US Navy SEALs (Sea, Air, Land) practice a beach assault; this would be done at night in wartime

(above right) An Israeli special forces soldier

(below) A US joint special forces team (from across the services) move out from a CV-22 Osprey whilst training in New Mexico, USA

FRIENDLY FIRE

'Blue-on 'blue' — Taking damage from your own side

DID YOU KNOW?
The term 'blue-on-blue' for friendly fire comes from NATO exercises of the 1960s to 1980s when NATO forces were marked blue and the enemy red

An especially bitter way to die

War is dangerous enough without worrying whether you are going to be hurt or killed by someone on your own side. But this is what so often happens in the confusion of a battlefield, sometimes called the 'fog of war.' Other reasons are being in the wrong position, errors in identification, and being 'trigger happy' caused by combat stress. These problems have been made worse by modern warfare where the distances involved between soldiers, aircraft and artillery can be significant and things can change very rapidly. The risk of friendly fire has been somewhat reduced by modern technology, including satellite navigation, radios/comms, and use of special electronics called IFF (Identification Friend or Foe). IFF is a unit which sends and receives signals so that your allies can identify that you are one of them. The messages are fed into computers to enable easy target identification. Nevertheless, incidents still sadly happen.

RAF Spitfire with black/white D-Day stripes used from June 1944 to prevent Allied aircraft being mistaken for Germans by 'friendly' ground troops

DID YOU KNOW?
The first RAF pilot to die in WW2 was shot down by a Spitfire. It was a case of mistaken identity

LEARNING POINT

Have your friends ever said or done something which has upset you? Perhaps you have done something in the past which has hurt loved ones in your family; I'm sure we all have.

How careful we should be not to cause any unnecessary hurt to others. Mistakes happen! Sometimes this hurt occurs without intending it, like friendly fire. Life is difficult enough as it is, without trouble between family and friends. We shouldn't want to hurt those who are really on our side. If we have hurt others through lack of care or selfishness, how important it is to try and make things better. We should also be ready to forgive others. So it is if you are a Christian and you are in a church. Satan likes nothing better than division and hurt between believers. How important it is to walk humbly and carefully, and forgive others! (Ephesians 4)

THE BIBLE SAYS . . .
'Confess your faults one to another, and pray one for another.' (James 5:16)

'Be ... kind one to another, ... forgiving one another.' (Ephesians 4:32)

(right) An A-10 Thunderbolt II destroys a target after firing a Maverick missile. Close Air Support (CAS) requires an aircraft to attack the enemy sometimes just a few hundred yards/metres from friendly troops, so the risk of friendly fire is high

(below) A chilling photo showing the moment a bomb ripped the tailplane off a 'friendly' during a raid over Berlin in 1944. The B-17 entered a spiral dive and crashed, killing all 11 on board

DID YOU KNOW?
It is estimated that between 2% and 25% of casualties in American wars are friendlies

COMBAT MEDICS

Giving life-saving treatment and getting to hospital—fast!

DID YOU KNOW?
In WW2, US medics had to remove their Red Cross markings as the Japanese troops tried extra hard to kill them

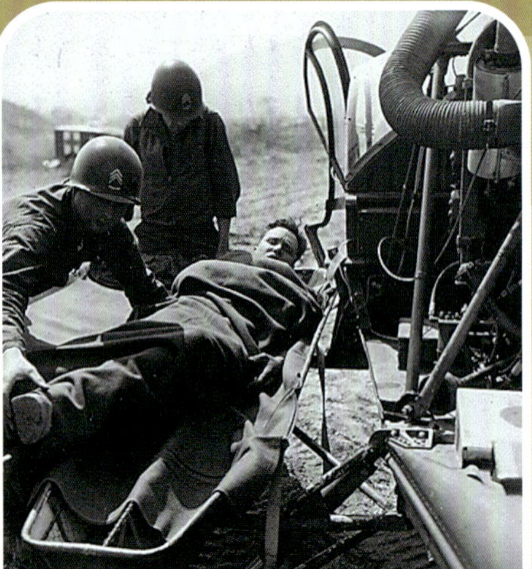

(above) A wounded US soldier is loaded onto the side of a helicopter, near the North Korean border, 1951; (below) Vehicles, ships, aircraft and troops used for helping the injured are often marked with the Red Cross symbol which means 'don't shoot at us'—based on an international agreement, the Geneva Convention

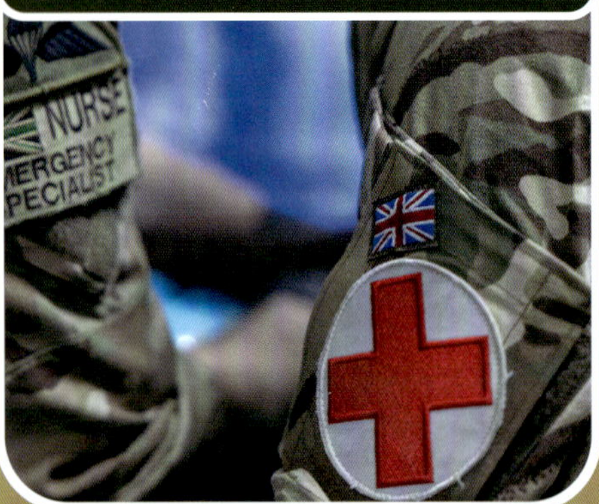

Get me out of here!

Combat medics are soldiers trained and equipped to go with troops to give life-saving treatment on the battlefield. It is especially important to control blood loss, manage pain, keep the heart beating and the spine/neck supported to prevent paralysis.

Injured soldiers need evacuating to hospital as quickly as possible as survival is much more likely with quick treatment (a principle known as the 'Golden Hour'). Since the Korean War (1950-1953), helicopters have been a key means for getting casualties out of difficult locations at speed. They also developed specialised mobile hospitals (known as M.A.S.H.—Mobile Army Surgical Hospitals) close to the front line.

LEARNING POINT

Why the hurry? Why should an army try so hard to rescue those who have life-threatening injuries and stop them dying? Wouldn't it be easier to just let them die and concentrate on looking after those who are well? Because life is precious. Man is God's special creation, made with His own hands (Genesis 2:7, Psalm 8:5); and he was created to reflect God's glory and likeness (Genesis 1:26-27). God said that life is so precious, that anyone who commits murder should lose his/her own life, showing the value God places on human life (Genesis 9:5-6). Finally, Man was created so that a countless number would be saved by Jesus and go to Heaven to be with Him for ever (Revelation 7:9-17); preserving life retains hope that one may live to hear the Gospel and be saved.

THE BIBLE SAYS . . .

'And God said, Let us make man in our image, after our likeness.' (Genesis 1:26)

'[God] *gives* to all life, and breath, and all things.' (Acts 17:25)

DID YOU KNOW?

The transport of injured troops is commonly known as 'casevac' (casualty evacuation—urgent from the battlefield) or 'medevac' (medical evacuation—planned)

(above) Israeli Air Force Special Forces rescue unit carry a stretcher to a waiting Blackhawk helicopter

(below left) A casualty is winched up through trees to a Huey helicopter, Vietnam, 1969

(below right) US Army combat medics in France, 1944

BRAVERY WITHOUT GUNS

Combat medics with faith who risked their lives to save others on the battlefield

World War 1 - John Gosden

At the outbreak of WW1, some Christians thought the war was just and others didn't. John Gosden could not in his conscience support the war but, being compelled to serve, he joined the Royal Army Medical Corps (RAMC). As a stretcher bearer, he would not be required to carry a gun—in fact, it was RAMC practice to go onto the battlefield unarmed. John was awarded the Military Medal for bravery because he had gone alone under heavy fire to tend a wounded soldier, and was wounded doing so.

John had faith that Jesus Christ was in it all; he rested in the peace made between God and man by Jesus' sacrifice on the cross. He was touched by the state of the men he helped, witnessing to them. As was common, he wrote letters to friends, especially to sympathise with those suffering. He wrote to parents after their son had been killed, 'The God of all comfort and consolation bless, console, comfort your hearts. I am grieved and afflicted with you, but helpless to do you good. God can and, I believe, will. With Christian love.'

DID YOU KNOW? The British Army had medical aid as early as the 1300s. The RAMC was formed in 1660

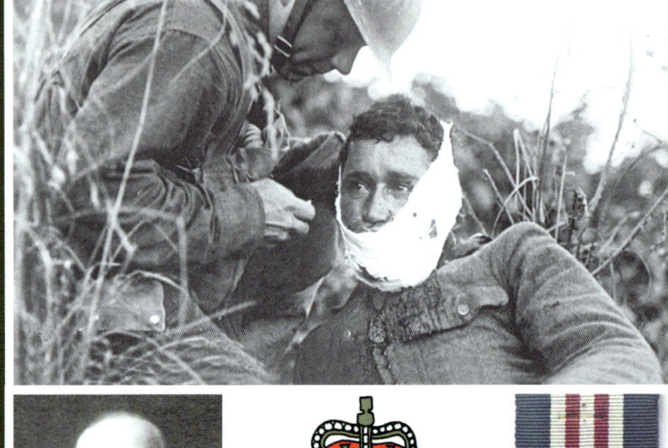

(top right) A US medic attends a wounded soldier, France, 1918; (centre) John Gosden / the Royal Army Medical Corps badge, translated as 'Faithful in adversity' / the Military Medal; (bottom right) stretcher bearers struggling with deep mud, Passchendaele, West Flanders, Belgium, 1917

(left to right) Doss in uniform; Doss on Hacksaw Ridge; President Truman awards the Medal of Honor

World War 2 - Desmond Doss

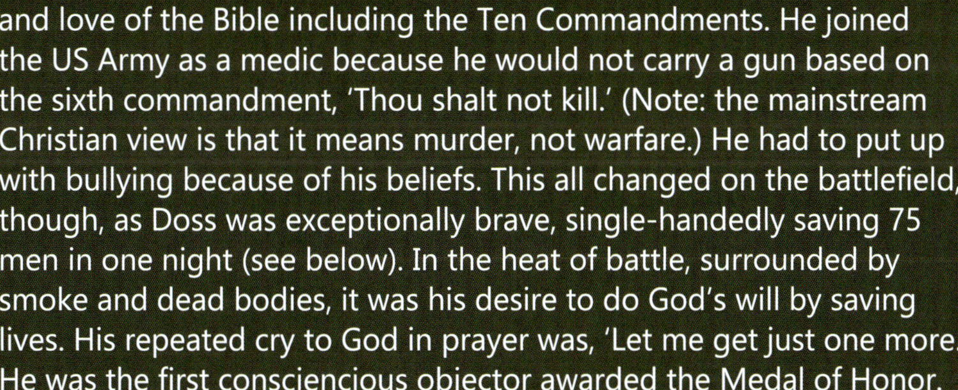

Desmond was a Seventh Day Adventist (see inset) with a sincere personal faith, and love of the Bible including the Ten Commandments. He joined the US Army as a medic because he would not carry a gun based on the sixth commandment, 'Thou shalt not kill.' (Note: the mainstream Christian view is that it means murder, not warfare.) He had to put up with bullying because of his beliefs. This all changed on the battlefield, though, as Doss was exceptionally brave, single-handedly saving 75 men in one night (see below). In the heat of battle, surrounded by smoke and dead bodies, it was his desire to do God's will by saving lives. His repeated cry to God in prayer was, 'Let me get just one more.' He was the first consciencious objector awarded the Medal of Honor.

Seventh Day Adventism is a Christian group which is by some considered a cult, though many beliefs are in line with mainstream Christianity. However, it follows Old Testament practices including keeping Saturday as a Sabbath day and some Jewish food laws.

Extract from the US Army's citation of his actions

'Doss was a company aid man when the 1st Battalion assaulted a jagged escarpment 400 feet high ['Hacksaw Ridge,' Okinawa]. As our troops gained the summit, heavy artillery, mortar and machine gun fire inflicted approx. 75 casualties and driving the others back. Doss refused to seek cover and remained in the fire-swept area with the many stricken, carrying them one by one to the edge of the escarpment and there lowering them to friendly hands. On 21 May, in a night attack, he remained in exposed territory while the rest of his company took cover, giving aid to the injured until he was himself seriously wounded in the legs by the explosion of a grenade [which he was kicking away from fellow soldiers]. Rather than call another aid man from cover, he cared for his own injuries and waited 5 hours before stretcher bearers reached him and started carrying him to cover. Doss, seeing a more critically wounded man nearby, crawled off the stretcher and directed the bearers to give their first attention to the other man. Awaiting the stretcher bearers' return, he was again struck, suffering a compound fracture of one arm. He bound a rifle to his shattered arm as a splint and then crawled 300 yards over rough terrain to the aid station. Through his outstanding bravery and unflinching determination in the face of desperately dangerous conditions Doss saved the lives of many soldiers. His name became a symbol throughout the 77th Infantry Division for outstanding gallantry far above and beyond the call of duty. [abridged]

DID YOU KNOW?
Doss's story was made into a motion picture, 'Hacksaw Ridge'

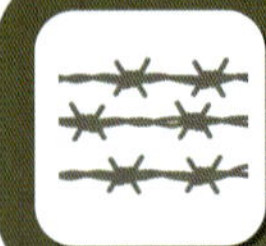

P.O.W.

Prisoners of War

Model of Stalag Luft III; Bushell's grave in Poland

THE GREAT ESCAPE

Arguably the most famous POW camp in the world is Stalag Luft III, built to house Allied airmen shot down over Europe. In March 1943, Squadron Leader Bushell masterminded a daring plan for 200 POWs to escape; each man would need false identity papers and a civilian outfit which had to be made in secret with limited supplies. They dug a tunnel 100 metres long but, unknown to them, it fell just short of the safety of the woods. They attempted the escape one night in March 1944, but after 80 men had escaped the Germans found out. Only 3 got to safety; 50 men were executed including Bushell.

Hope sets you free

In ancient times it was common for men captured in battle to be slaughtered, but there were exceptions; for example God's directions to Moses (and Joshua) to spare the men who surrendered to the Israelites (Deuteronomy 20:10-15); and the actions of Israel when the captured Syrian Army was fed and let go (2 Kings 6:22-23, which hints that taking POWs was not uncommon for them). Since the time of the Reformation, in Europe attitudes started changing towards POWs; after a treaty was signed in 1648 it was common for them to be returned after a war. In WW2, despite the Nazis' horrific treatment of Jews and Russians, 'western' Allied POWs were generally respected by them. In the Far East, it was not the case with the Japanese; Allied POWs were barely fed, cruelly treated, denied medicine and aid, and worked to death in the jungle.

LEARNING POINT

One of the most remarkable books I have ever read is 'Miracle on the River Kwai' by Ernest Gordon, a Scotsman in the British Army in WW2. It recounts his time as a POW in Thailand, forced to work on the Death Railway with his fellows dropping dead all around him from exhaustion and illness. He tells how the camp had an air of hopelessness and death—that is, until two Christians, 'Dusty' and 'Dinty,' lovingly nursed him when ill and close to death, talking to Him about Jesus. It so affected Ernest that, despite weakness, pain, exhaustion, and hunger, he no longer felt despair, but instead a love for others and a desire to help them. He came to faith in Jesus, started leading Bible studies and doing things for others. Eventually, a church was formed in the camp, and the whole atmosphere changed to one of hope—not in their outward circumstances——but an inward hope based on Jesus' gift of peace in the heart (John 14:27, Romans 5:1).

THE BIBLE SAYS . . .

'Now the God of hope fill you with joy and peace in believing ... through the power of the Holy Ghost [Spirit].' (Romans 15:13)

DID YOU KNOW?

The earliest known purpose-built POW camp was in Huntingdonshire, England in 1797

DID YOU KNOW?
The Germans captured 5.7 million Russians as POWs in WW2, 60% of which died

DID YOU KNOW?
The phrase 'Prisoner of War' was first recorded in 1610

(top left) Russian soldiers surrendering to the Germans, 1942; (top right) Russian POW near the Arctic Circle, Finland, 1940; (centre left) the notorious Nazi Heinrich Himmler inspecting Russian POWs, 1941; (below left) the site of the escape tunnel, Stalag Luft III POW camp in Poland; (centre right) Australian and Dutch POWs captured by the Japanese suffering from Beri Beri through lack of food; (bottom right) Kanchanaburi war cemetery, Thailand, with the graves of those who died building the notorious 'Death Railway' between Burma and Thailand

SACRIFICE

Paying the ultimate price—your own life

What is love?

In society today, most people think love is a fuzzy romantic feeling. In truth, it is putting aside your own desires for the good of others.

Men have gone to war because they felt it was right—loving, even—to sacrifice their own comforts and safety to protect family, community, their own nation and others. Sadly, even in the 20th Century (1900-1999), millions have paid the ultimate price—with their life — sometimes in selfless acts to protect comrades; at other times, commanders have sacrificed men to achieve some strategic aim.

LEARNING POINT

The Bible says that without love (or 'charity') even the ultimate sacrifice of laying down your life is not enough (1 Corinthians 13:3); but what a difference love makes! Jesus said that there is no greater demonstration of love than dying for others, if it is truly done *in love*. Jesus Himself is the ultimate fulfilment of His own saying. No-one has ever suffered like Jesus, when He was forsaken by His Father and willingly went to a crushingly painful and humiliating death so that all who believe on Him would have liberty and live for ever. *That* is love.

THE BIBLE SAYS . . .

'Greater love *has* no man than this, that a man lay down his life for his friends.' (John 15:13)

Tyne Cot, Ypres, Belgium: the largest Commonwealth war cemetery in the world with 11,965 graves, of which 8,369 are unnamed as the men could not be identified

Abide with me; fast falls the eventide;
The darkness deepens; Lord with me abide.
When other helpers fail and comforts flee,
Help of the helpless, O abide with me.

Swift to its close ebbs out life's little day;
Earth's joys grow dim; its glories pass away;
Change and decay in all around I see;
O Thou who changest not, abide with me.

I need Thy presence every passing hour.
What but Thy grace can foil the tempter's power?
Who, like Thyself, my guide and stay can be?
Through cloud and sunshine, Lord, abide with me.

I fear no foe, with Thee at hand to bless;
Ills have no weight, and tears no bitterness.
Where is death's sting? Where, grave, thy victory?
I triumph still, if Thou abide with me.

Henry Francis Lyte 1793-1847

This hymn, written when the author was dying, is sung at Remembrance Day services. It is based on the request of two disciples in Luke 24:29: 'Abide wit us: for it is toward evening ... And [Jesus] went in.'

WILLIAM
FREDERICK
LIEBENOW
LCDR US NAVY
WORLD WAR II
JAN 18 1920
FEB 24 2017
SILVER STAR

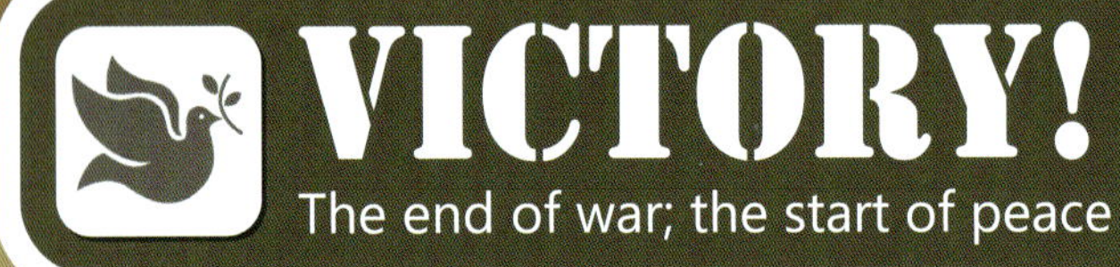

VICTORY!

The end of war; the start of peace

DID YOU KNOW?
The First World War ceasefire took effect at the 11th hour of the 11th day of the 11th month, i.e. 11am, 11 November 1918

Painting of the Germans formerly surrendering to the Allies at the end of the First World War, 11 November 1918

Winners and Losers

The reason for going to war is (or should be) to win; all effort must be directed at that aim. The most powerful side has the victory, and the vanquished (defeated) are at the victor's mercy. When hostilities cease, how joyful everyone involved should be! The main danger is past, Prisoners of War can be freed, troops can return home, and families can be reunited. Although the sorrow of losing others may remain, and soldiers may still be suffering PTSD, life can start to return to the way it should be, perhaps the way it was before the war.

LEARNING POINT

When Jesus died on the cross and rose again, He conquered death and Satan (1 Corinthians 15:55), in the biggest victory of all time. But in His wisdom He allows the battle of life to rage on, and it will do so until the end of time. The Bible says that Christians already have a victory in measure (1 John 5:4), but the victory will be total in that last great day when Jesus will return to take His people home to be with Him forever in Heaven. (Who are His people? All who feel their need of Jesus; see Revelation 22:17.) He will wipe away every tear from their eyes, and there will be no more sadness, pain or death (Revelation 21:4). He will give them a crown (a symbol of power) and they will reign with Him. Everything will be restored to perfection like the Garden of Eden before Satan started warring against God (Revelation 2:7). What rejoicing there will be in Heaven, what songs of victory! (Revelation 5:9)

And what will happen to Satan, his demons, and all those who did not believe on the Son of God? Solemnly, they will be judged for their rebellion and sin and cast into outer darkness, with no hope of ever getting to Heaven (Revelation 20:11-15). God is perfect; nothing can enter Heaven which would ruin it (Revelation 21:27).

THE BIBLE SAYS . . .

'We are more than conquerors through him [Jesus] that loved us.' (Romans 8:37)

'Death is swallowed up in victory.' (1 Corinthians 15:54)

None of us deserve Heaven, or anything good. But God in His mercy and love has made a way of salvation in His only Son, Jesus Christ. Are you thankful that there is free salvation, though purchased at great cost? (Isaiah 55:1, Isaiah 53:5)

DID YOU KNOW?
VE-Day was short for 'Victory in Europe' Day; VJ-Day was 'Victory in Japan' Day (i.e. the Pacific Theatre)

(top, left to right) VE-Day celebrations, end of WW2, May 1945: military personnel celebrating in London; a street party in Swansea, Wales; Winston Churchill gives his famous 'V for Victory salute. (bottom) HMS Invincible returns home to Portsmouth after the victory in the Falkland Islands, 1982

GLOSSARY

Doing battle with new 'military' words?

'They gave their tomorrow for our today'

'We will remember them'

Sentiments expressed on Remembrance Day

Allied/Allies: The UK, British Empire, USA, Soviet Union and other countries 'allied' together in *WW2* to fight the *Axis* powers.

Ammunition: Cartridges (rounds), grenades & shells fired by guns.

Artillery: Big guns which fire large shells; modern ones can fire many miles/kilometres and are towed by trucks or are self-propelled.

Aviator: (an alternative to *airmen*) Pilots and other aircrew responsible for flying and operating aircraft including helicopters.

Axis: Germany, Japan, Italy, etc. fighting the *Allies* in *WW2*.

Bayonet: A pointed blade on the front of a rifle for stabbing.

Camouflage: Colours and patterns applied to clothing, equipment, weapons, machines and skin to blend in with the surroundings.

Casualty: A soldier (or sailor or airman) wounded or killed in battle.

SA80 rifle (p79) ammunition rounds made up of *bullet* (the pointed bit which is fired) and *casing* (ejected from the side of the weapon)

Civilian: ('civvy') Someone who is not in the military. Non-military clothing may be referred to as 'civvies.'

Cold War: The period when western (*NATO*) and eastern (*Warsaw Pact*) countries were on the brink of war, with both sides suspicious that the other would start a war. It was notable for use of nuclear weapons as a deterrent against the other side attacking. It started after *WW2* and ended in 1991.

Conscription: When a government requires men (and women) to join the military, or be punished.

Crusades: A series of military expeditions from Europe to the Middle East in the 12th and 13th Centuries to attempt to liberate the Christians in Jerusalem and the 'Holy Land' from the occupying Muslim forces.

Corps: (pronounced 'core') From the French for 'body,' meaning an organised military unit.

Desert (to)/deserter: To run away from active military duty, without permission to do.

Drill: Marching and other moves (e.g. saluting, rifle handling, standing to 'attention' or 'at ease') undertaken by a squad in a precisely timed and coordinated way, following orders. Drill often forms part of a parade when soldiers are inspected by senior officers or officials.

Field (in the): Out in the countryside, desert, jungle, moors, woods etc. i.e. away from military bases.

Front line(s): The extent of land under your control, and where you are closest to the enemy.

Grenade: A small explosive weapon thrown by hand, shot from a rifle attachment, or fired from a launcher.

HMS: His (or Her) Majesty's Ship; title given to warships of the (British) Royal Navy.

Marksman/marksmanship: Someone proven skilful in shooting a gun accurately; good at hitting a target.

Military: Someone or something related to the armed forces (army, navy, air force, space force).

NATO: North Atlantic Treaty Organisation, a group of 'western' nations allied together after World War 2.
Parade Ground: Normally a cleared or paved area, where soldiers can drill or be on parade (see earlier).
Personnel: Men or women in the military available for active duty.
Propaganda: Information spread by a government to discourage the enemy, build morale amongst military personnel and civilians, and build support for its actions amongst the population over which they have power. Propaganda is often associated with half-truths, omitting key information and even lies.
Radar / radar signature / radar cross-section: A device which emits a strong electrical pulse into the air, which bounces back off an object, and is returned to the radar where it is picked up. The electronics in the radar can identify direction and distance of enemy or friendly aircraft, ships etc. The radar signature is the distinctive radar return sent back from an aircraft or ship allowing it to be identified. The radar cross-section is how large the aircraft appears to the radar rather than how large it actually is. Modern stealth aircraft aim to have the smallest radar cross-section possible.
RAF: The (British) Royal Air Force, the oldest independent air force in the world (not being responsible to an army or navy), formed from the (British Army) Royal Flying Corps and Royal Naval Air Service in 1918.
Remembrance Day: 11th November or nearest Sunday; a day to remember those who have lost their lives in conflicts especially of both World Wars. Many wear poppies, a tradition started after WW1 because poppies grew on the battle sites in Belgium after the war. Two minutes silence is observed at 11am.

Veterans at a Remembrance Day parade, Bristol, 2019

Rifle: Long-barrelled gun with a spiral groove cut inside which spins the bullet so it fires more accurately.
Scramble: Aircraft taking off as soon as possible to intercept an enemy, usually in 2-5 minutes from alert.
Shell: Ammunition fired by a large gun where the bullet contains an explosive or other deadly filling.
Stretcher bearers: Those who carry (bear) a stretcher to move the injured, normally from the battlefield.
USS: United States Ship, a ship of the US Navy.
Veteran: Someone who has served in the military, but has since left (been demobilised, or 'demobbed').
Warsaw Pact: Agreement signed in 1955 between the Soviet Union and Eastern European countries: Poland, East Germany, Czechoslovakia, Hungary, Romania, Bulgaria and Albania. Formed to counter *NATO*, it was disbanded in 1991 when the Soviet Union collapsed. Countries in Eastern Europe at this time were said to be behind the Iron Curtain, as one could not easily get in or out.
WW1: World War 1, the First World War, the Great War, 1914-1918.
WW2: World War 2, the Second World War, 1939-1945.

DID YOU KNOW?
The longest conflict in history was the 'Reconquista,' recovering Spain and Portugal from Muslim invaders, at 774 years long (718-1492 AD)

Published by: Day One Publications, Ryelands Rd, Leominster, HR6 8NZ
sales@dayone.co.uk
www.dayone.co.uk

Answers to questions on page 57:

1. Moses / strong wind / Pharaoh & army
2. Deborah (and Barak) / river flooding / Jabin, Sisera (and their army with 900 iron chariots)
3. Gideon / enemy panic / Midianites, Amalekites, Children of the East
4. Samson / supernatural strength / Philistines
5. Jonathan / prophecy & courage / Philistines (Philistine camp/garrison of soldiers)
6. David / courage and skill / Goliath
7. Elisha / blindness / Syrian army
8. Elisha / imagining noise / Syrian army
9. Isaiah / Angel of the LORD / Assyrian army

(right) Men of K Company, 42 Commando Royal Marines ready to board a RAF CH-47 Chinook transport helicopter as they return from duty in Helmand Province, Afghanistan, 2006

ISBN 978-1-84625-803-9

Bible quotes are from the Authorised (King James) Version. If words have been replaced for clarity, these are shown in *italics*. If words have been inserted, these are shown in square brackets [ ].

Reference to organisations or persons does not imply endorsement by the Author or Publisher of their views or activities. Likewise, inclusion of an organisation or individual does not imply their endorsement of this book or its contents.

DayOne

ACKNOWLEDGEMENTS

Recognising help given and the sources of the images in this book

Key: p=page number pp=pages T=top B=bottom L=left R=right C=centre

SASRA Soldiers' and Aviators' Scripture Readers Association https://www.sasra.org.uk

Thanks to Warren and Sian for supplying all images (© SASRA) and for their help in producing the SASRA feature on pp30-31.

UK Ministry of Defence (MoD) / Open Government License, UK (OGL) www.defenceimagery.mod.uk

Images reproduced under the Open Government Licence (OGL), http://www.nationalarchives.gov.uk/open-government-license/version/3/. This section confirms that the the following images are © Crown Copyright [year] whilst those downloaded via **Wikimedia Commons** are suffixed [W] with the relevant older version of the OGL also included in the brackets, and those downloaded from **Flickr** suffixed [F] with CC license in brackets (see below for Flickr and CC website and license details).

Front cover T Cpl Si Longworth RLC (2014) [W,2]; B Sgt Brian Gamble (2003) [W,1]; pp2-3 Cpl Tom Evans (2018) [W]; Camo background on pp4-5+p57+Back Cover B Cpl Adrian Harlen RLC (2009) [W,1]; p6 LA(Phot) Will Haigh (2012) [F, SA2]; p13 main image SAC Katrina Cox (2022); CR Sgt Matty Matthews; p19T Sgt Rob Kane (2024); pp20-21 Sgt Donald C Todd (2023); p22T Sgt Andy Malthouse ABIPP (2007) [W,1]; B LPhot Barry Swainsbury; p24 Dominic King (2016); B AS1 Tomas Barnard (2023); Inset LPhot Johnson (2022); p27T Cpl Rebecca Brown RLC (2024); B LCpl Lucy Aslett (2024); p28BC Sgt Donald C Todd (2024); BR Sgt Rupert Frere (2017) [W,1]; p37CR LPhot Dan Rosenbaum; p38 Inset POA(Phot) Gaz Ames (2009); pp38-39 UK MOD (2022); p40 CB (Typhoons) AS1 Jason Russell (2024); p41TR Sgt Matthews (2024); p43L AS1 Amber Mayall (2024); p45L PO Phot Arron Hoare (2023); Inset LPhot Stainer-Hutchins (2025); TR Cpl Nanda Atherton RLC (2024); CR Cpl Aaron J Stone (2023); p46C UK MOD (2022); p47BL UK MOD (2013); p49B Sgt Donald C Todd RLC (2022); p51TL Cpl Aaron J Stone (2024); B POA(Phot) Sean Clee (2011); p53BR Sgt Anthony Boocock RLC (2008); p64BR Sgt Anil Gurung RLC (2025); p73B Royal Navy (1982); p74 (ammo) POA(Phot) Dave Jenkins (2011) [W,1]; p75 Shawn Spencer-Smith [F,ND]; pp76-77 POA(Phot) Sean Clee (2006); p79 Stuart Hill / UK MOD (2017) [W]; Back cover TL Sgt Ben Beale; TR Cpl Paul Saxby RAF; CL Cpl Nathan Tanuku.

Government Open Data License—India (GODL)

This image is reproduced under the GODL—India, https://data.gov.in/sites/default/files/Gazette_Notification_OGDL.pdf: p29BR Defense Research and Development Organisation (2013). Source https://commons.wikimedia.org/

US Department of Defense (DoD) www.defense.gov/Multimedia/Photos/

Thanks to the US DoD for making images available in the public domain used throughout this book. The appearance of DoD visual information does not imply or constitute DoD endorsement.

Wikimedia Commons / Flickr https://commons.wikimedia.org + www.flickr.com
Licensed by Creative Commons www.creativecommons.org/licenses

License details available at above web address. Unless noted in square brackets after each attribution, image license will be 'CC BY 2.0'; abbreviations are used where the license type differs: SA='CC BY-SA 2.0'; ND='CC BY-ND 2.0'; 3='CC BY-3.0', etc. All photos have been sourced from Wikimedia Commons except those suffixed [F] sourced from Flickr.

p9TL Peter Sladek [SA3]; p9CL Guenter Konz-Beyer; TR J Barcena [F,ND2]; B Peter Gronemann; p10T Discombobulates [SA4]; BL PR department Parliament of Latvia [F,SA]; BR Estonian Foreign Ministry [F]; CL Damien Everett [F]; p19BL Thomas Quine [F]; BCL James Boyes [F]; p23 All British Army Insignia by Sodacan; p28 TL Snake3yes [F]; TC Rawpixel [SA4]; TR EmDee [3]; BL Kmtextor [SA4]; p29TL Bundeswehr-Fotos; TR Oren Rozen [3]; BL Tim (Airwolfhound) [F,SA]; BC Michael Garlick [SA]; p40T Tim (Airwolfhound) [F,SA]; CT+TL Tim (Airwolfhound) [F,SA] [F,SA]; p41B Amy Felce [F,ND]; p47BR New York National Guard [F,ND]; p55B Ian Harris

BRITISH ARMY SA80-A2 FULLY-AUTOMATIC ASSAULT RIFLE

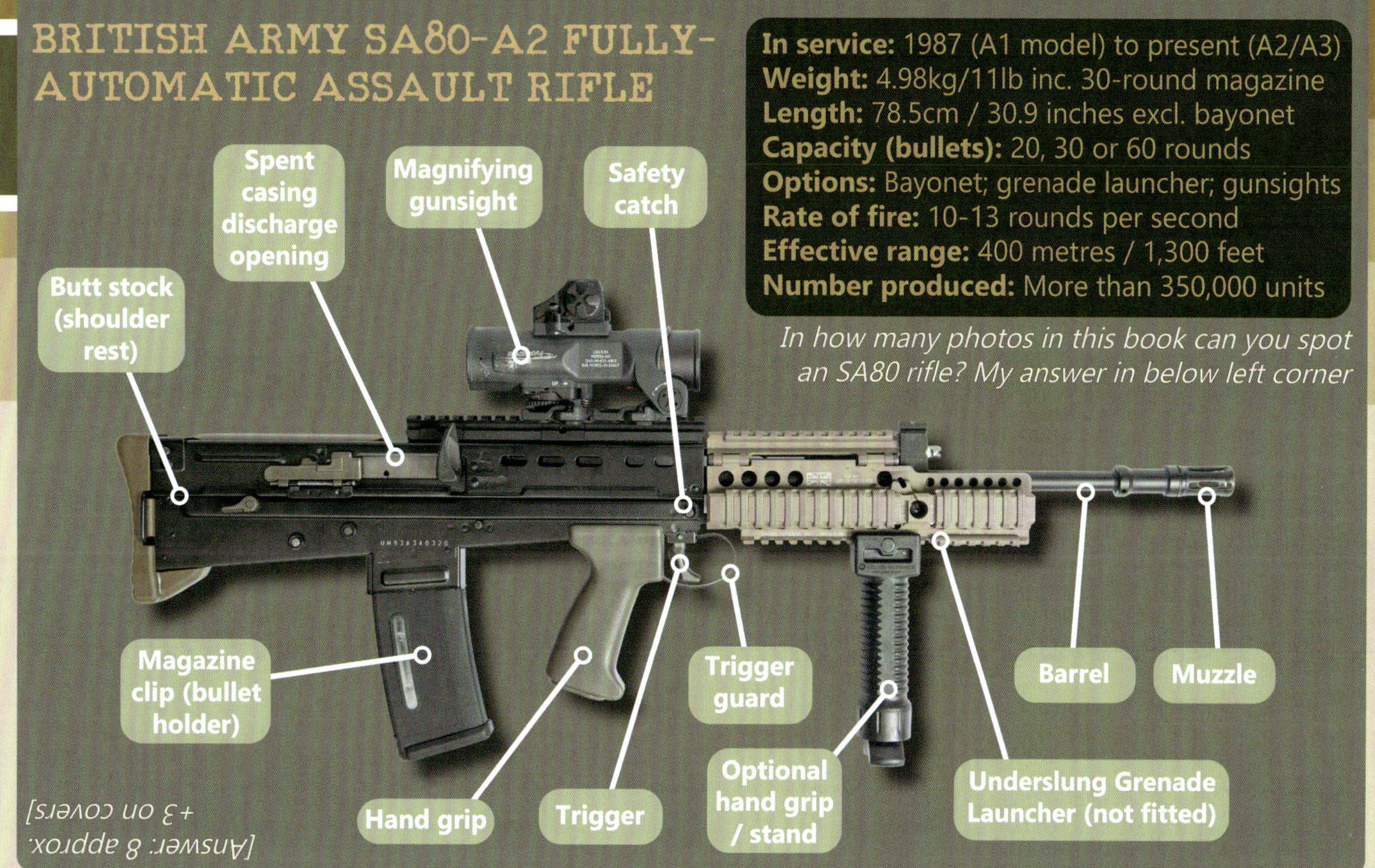

In service: 1987 (A1 model) to present (A2/A3)
Weight: 4.98kg/11lb inc. 30-round magazine
Length: 78.5cm / 30.9 inches excl. bayonet
Capacity (bullets): 20, 30 or 60 rounds
Options: Bayonet; grenade launcher; gunsights
Rate of fire: 10-13 rounds per second
Effective range: 400 metres / 1,300 feet
Number produced: More than 350,000 units

In how many photos in this book can you spot an SA80 rifle? My answer in below left corner

[Answer: 8 approx. +3 on covers]

[F,ND]; p56 Arnold Reinhold [SA4]; p59 Inset Raimond Spekking [SA4]; B Alan Wilson [F,SA]; p60T (red badge) Gjw9999 [SA4]; p61TR Israeli Defense Forces; p62 Derek Finch [F]; p63TR 99th Air Base Wing Public Affairs Photographers [F,ND]; p65T IDF Spokesperson's Unit [SA3]; BL John F. Bauer [SA4]; p66CR Hsq7278 [SA4]; p68T Kieran Lamb [F,SA]; TR Finnish Wartime Photograph Archive [4]; C Adsk [SA3]; p69TL Konok Tamas (fortepan) [SA3]; BR PA [SA3]; p70 Mike Thurston [F,SA]; p73TC SteveR [F].

Icons from the Noun Project https://thenounproject.com (items marked '~' also appear on p7)

Footer icon Tank by arista septiana dewi; p4 envelope open by Pericon Design; p8~ middle by Adrien Coquet; p10~ alliance by Adrien Coquet; p12~ signature by Humam; p16~ army shoes by icongarage; p18~ police by Nicky Spencer; p22~ rank by DTDesign; p24~ Gym by Djoelikatin; p28~ Swords by iconblast; p30 open book by Yosua Bungaran; p32~ Nuclear by Rikas Dzihab; p36~ Submarine by Taewon Kang; p40~ Cloud by Mila Karmila; p40-41 (6 no.): hidden by Rizalwale; Chameleon by sentya irma; quiet by Tyler Gobberdiel; Thermometer by Vectors Point; Radar by ArashDesign; measuring tape by Kosong Tujuh; p44~ camp by sandiindra; p46~ Food by Tony; p48~ cornet by Creative Stall; p50~ soldier helmet by Vectors Market; p52~ explosion by Aldric Rodríguez; p58~ stranger by Daniil Churakov; p66 Gun by Danang Marhendra; p68~ Barbed Wire by Ishaq_hmad; p70~ Grave by Andrejs Kirma; p72~ peace dove by Luis Prado.

Many thanks: Colin Easton for the photos of my Great Uncles Cyril, Billy and Harold on p4, and Dad for the photo of Great Uncle Reg. Thanks to Dad, Andy & Joanna T., Andy R., Tim A., Lily P. and Josh & Grace A. who reviewed the draft (Proverbs 27:17).

A US Navy F/A-18E Super Hornet being prepared for launch from the USS Harry S. Truman aircraft carrier, 2025. The steam is from the catapult launch system